ADMIRAL RICHARD E. BYRD

LIVES TO REMEMBER

Books by Alfred Steinberg

ELEANOR ROOSEVELT

DANIEL WEBSTER

Admiral
Richard E. Byrd

by Alfred Steinberg

ILLUSTRATED BY CHARLES BECK

G. P. PUTNAM'S SONS
NEW YORK

© 1960 by Alfred Steinberg

All rights reserved

Library of Congress Catalog
Card Number: 60-6914

MANUFACTURED IN THE UNITED STATES OF AMERICA

VAN REES PRESS • NEW YORK

Published simultaneously in the Dominion of Canada by
Longmans, Green and Company, Toronto

CONTENTS

FOR LISE—

MY ADVENTUROUS ONE

ADMIRAL RICHARD E. BYRD

Chapter 1

A BOY AND HIS DREAMS

At the tail end of December, 1955, a small band of
American explorers scrambled over the edge of
the high ice barrier wall onto the immense white continent of Antarctica. The day was raw and their footing
unsure, but they considered these inconveniences minor.
For they had made their way to this forsaken spot on an

important mission. They had come to dedicate a base to be known as Little America V.

If there was one man among them whose every move stamped him as leader, it was a slender, handsome man with alert blue eyes. He was Admiral Richard Evelyn Byrd, whose name stands today at the summit of his country's leading explorers. It was he who provided the driving force for this undertaking.

Almost thirty years before, he had taken off from almost this very place to become the first man in history to fly over the South Pole, some 800 miles away. On four previous expeditions he had established Little Americas here and had led explorers to this ice-age continent to unlock its frozen secrets. Now standing proudly as the Stars and Stripes crackled in the harsh wind, he presented an old-fashioned picture as he wore the same knee-high boots and fur headpiece he had worn on his first expedition in 1928.

However, this was more than a sentimental gesture on his part. Through the old, Admiral Byrd could measure how far he had traveled in fulfilling his dream of half a lifetime, to claim a continent for his country. He knew that six other American bases, including one at the South Pole itself, would soon spring up in the Antarctic. Some would become permanent bases, essential in giving the United States clear title to those areas. Almost as important to him, hundreds of scientists from eleven other nations would also be descending upon the Antarctic. They planned to swing the door open wide on his own earlier research there in glaciology, meteorology, magnetism, astronomy, and a host of other earth sciences.

"Admiral of the Antarctic" was the title bestowed upon him throughout the world. To millions his name spelled adventure, discovery, and bravery. Others also hailed him as "Admiral of the Ends of the Earth." For he had conquered the Arctic as well, with his pioneering first flight across the North Pole.

Yet there was little in Richard Byrd's family background to give any inkling that he would one day become his country's greatest explorer.

Richard Evelyn Byrd was born on October 25, 1888, in the quiet town of Winchester, Virginia. The Byrds of Virginia were among the first families of the Old Dominion State. Aristocratic Colonel William Byrd was one of the earliest settlers when he arrived at the James River about 1670. His son, William Byrd II, founded the city of Richmond and had money enough to support a private 500-man army to protect his vast landholdings from Indian forays. Through following generations, the Byrds stood for tradition and genteel dignity.

However, long before Dick was born the family fortune had taken a sharp downward turn. By the close of the Civil War, the Byrd lands were in the hands of others and the attic trunks were filled with worthless Confederate money. Dick's father, who was also Richard Evelyn Byrd, was a quiet, scholarly man with an aristocratic air. On an average of three hours each day, he devoted himself to the study of philosophy, literature, and science. He detested politics, yet in order to support his wife and three sons, he spent almost his entire adult life in public affairs. A short, bespectacled man, carelessly dressed but with a grand manner, he put his cultured voice to use as his county's prosecuting attorney for twenty years. He also served three terms as Speaker of the Virginia Assembly at the capitol in Richmond, and as Assistant U. S. Attorney General under his old college classmate, President Woodrow Wilson. Once when he was assured of becoming his state's next governor, he turned down the offer with a loud "No!"

On his mother's side, Dick was a direct descendant of Lord Delaware. Her family, too, was impoverished by the Civil War. Like the Byrds, Eleanor Bolling Flood's family made its mark in politics, and produced ambassadors, a United States Senator and a key member of the House of Representatives.

From the start, Dick Byrd was different from the general Byrd pattern. Some said he resembled Grandpa Colonel William Byrd, a swashbuckling Confederate officer, who was given up for dead in the Civil War. Long afterward, it was he who came galloping into his farmyard and called out to his saddened wife, "Does the widow Byrd live here?"

Undersized and thin, young Dick nevertheless made up for his slight figure by his mischievous nature and courage. "Foolish deviltries," his scholarly father indignantly called his many escapades. With his little dog Judy, Dick was forever off on one adventure or another, roving in the Shenandoah Valley and the Blue Ridge Mountains.

On one occasion when he was ten, an old man told him about a big cave "across the mountains, down the valley, across the fields close to the river. The cave is as big as all of Winchester," said the old man, spreading his arms wide.

Early the next morning Dick and Judy set off for the

cave, which did not actually exist. By nightfall when he and his dog started back for far-off Winchester, a torrential rain began. In the woods where the two sought shelter, lightning almost jarred loose a huge tree near them. With the river swollen and the big bridge washed away, a dozen search parties combed the area for Dick in vain. Almost at dawn when hope for his safety had disappeared, he and Judy crept exhausted and drenched into the house.

Another time while visiting family friends at Hampton Roads, he induced them to let him take their sailboat out, even though he had never sailed before. In the face of a rising storm, he sailed across the bay and back, barely managing a safe return. While his father choked at this display of foolhardiness, his mother merely shook her head and sighed. "Richard was born an adventurer and explorer," she said. "He is absolutely without fear."

It was true that he did not know the meaning of fear. In fact, this was to remain one of his chief characteristics throughout his life. Once he dived fully clothed into a wild ocean to haul in a sailor who had been swept overboard.

Actually, few of Dick's carryings-on surprised his father, though the results often raised his blood pressure. Coming home from a hard day in court, he gasped to discover that Dick had dug up the precious front lawn to build a trench. The colorful garden in the rear also disappeared as the price for erecting a sturdy fort.

There was even an occasion when Dick's reputation almost killed his father. Racing his horse into his dirt driveway one afternoon, the elder Byrd leaped from his carriage at the sight of his burning stable. Unable to find

Dick anywhere, he burst past the arms of the fire brigade and rushed inside to rescue his son. When he emerged from the stable after a complete search, his clothes were on fire and he was badly burned. Dick was found sound asleep under the couch in the back parlor of the house.

There were three Byrd brothers. But luckily two fitted into the normal Byrd pattern on most occasions. Tom, Dick, and Harry they were, with quiet Harry the oldest and husky Tom the youngest. The citizens of Winchester likened them to the Three Musketeers because of the way they came to each other's aid in emergencies. When a bully taunted studious Harry, he found himself tackled by little Dick and pummeled by Tom.

Displeased with his puny body, Dick made a continuous effort to build himself up physically. He ran, swam, boxed and rode horseback. He revealed no interest in any sport unless he could participate and not be a spectator. Poor Tom, who was well on the way to his eventual height of six feet two inches, found himself bedeviled by his smaller older brother who challenged him in a long series of events. They dived for coins, wrestled and raced, with Dick victorious in almost all tests.

Once when they wrestled and Dick rubbed Tom's nose in the dirt, Tom grew enraged and chased Dick into the bathroom. With the door locked on him, Tom began chopping at the door with a knife. Dick boosted himself out the window, slid down the drainpipe and ran three miles to Dr. Love, the family doctor. "Please come right away, Dr. Love," he appealed between gasps. "Tom has gone crazy."

But there was another side to Dick. When he wasn't

off on an adventure, he could be found devouring his father's books on the classics and history. The elder Byrd was often astonished by the breadth of the young boy's mind. He sometimes wondered whether Dick would be influenced particularly by any one book on his library shelf.

There was one such book, but it came from outside the house. The Christmas when Dick was eleven, Grandpa Flood gave him a book which dealt with explorers. The title was *Explorers and Travelers*. Hungrily reading its pages, Dick came across the story of Elisha Kent Kane, an American doctor and explorer who sailed into the Arctic Ocean twice during the 1850's. The first Kane venture was in 1850 when he went along as a member of the Grinnell Expedition in a fruitless search for a lost British explorer named Sir John Franklin. In 1853, Kane led his own expedition and reached the northernmost point attained up to that time.

Dreamy-eyed, Dick thrilled to Dr. Kane's adventures. He walked the dusty streets of Winchester with a new determination. One day he would be the first to reach the North Pole! Indeed he scrawled this vow later in his diary and even drew diagrams of the equipment he planned to take with him.

The elder Byrd was amused by the boy's fired-up enthusiasm. Nevertheless, he scoffed at the prophecy of Dick's great-grandmother that one day a Byrd would be famous for his polar explorations. Dick would go into law or become a farmer. Exploring was merely a childish whim, and Dick's father was certain it would be cast aside and be replaced by the hero of the next book Dick read. At the moment he was more concerned with reports that Dick had passed several friends by with a dreamy expression on his face and had failed to recognize them. What had happened to the traditional Byrd reputation for good manners?

Perhaps Dick's fancy for travel and adventure might have died a quick death if Adam "Kit" Carson had not existed. Carson, who was a lawyer associated with Dick's father, sported a long black mustache, merry eyes and an enthusiastic grin. Kit joined little Dick in many games and the boy worshiped him.

When the United States went to war with Spain in 1898 to free Cuba and the Philippine Islands, Kit served as captain with the Virginia Fourth Volunteers. When the war was over in 1899, Captain Carson invited Dick to march in review with the Fourth Volunteers before President William McKinley in Washington. Dick wore a cut-down officer's uniform and marched at the head of the parade. So mindful was he of his responsibility that when he passed the President's stand he kept his eyes straight ahead. The result was that he did not return the personal salute McKinley gave him. The crowd roared and Dick's face turned red when he learned of his omission.

Afterward, Captain Carson and the Fourth Volunteers were sent to the Philippines where an insurrection had broken out against the American liberators. Once in the Philippines, Carson won promotion to major and then he became a district judge of the provinces south of Manila on Luzon Island.

In July, 1902, a letter came addressed to Dick from Judge Carson. How would Dick like to visit him in the Philippines?

"I could hardly believe my ears," his mother told his father. "But I soon learned that Richard was for accepting the invitation in all seriousness. He even hinted he would run away if he wasn't given permission."

There would be none of this nonsense, his father insisted. No boy only thirteen years old was old enough to travel halfway around the world unattended. Besides, the rebels were still shooting at Americans in the Philippines and deadly cholera was rampant there.

But his father underestimated the boy's stubbornness. Daily, Dick persisted in a relentless campaign. Finally worn down by his pleas, his parents gave their reluctant consent. The Winchester *Star* heralded the decision with the following lines:

> Dick is perhaps the youngest person to take such a long journey alone. He is a manly and handsome youth, plucky and aggressive and as brave as a lion.

However, he was not so manly or handsome on August 9 when his tearful mother bade him farewell at the train station at Washington, D.C. He had all he could do to pretend he was not sad. In addition, his eyes were almost swollen shut with poison oak. But once the train started off for San Francisco, he thought only of the adventure ahead. "I had a suitcase, all shiny and new," he recalled. "And I had quietly slipped in special treasures, such as a big jackknife and a ball of string."

Alone he traveled to the West Coast, where he boarded the *Sumner,* an Army transport vessel. The first port of call was Nagasaki, Japan, but in the China Seas the vessel

almost fell apart in a typhoon. During the terror, Dick
was assigned by the captain to care for a frightened school-
teacher. Later he wrote his father:

> I am not going to write a long letter because I know
> you do not like to read them. The day after I wrote
> mama a letter we had a big typhoon. I tell you it was
> a bad one. It delayed us two days and carried us 250
> miles out of our way. . . . One lady got so frightened
> she came near dying. The ship rocked so much that we
> could not eat anything in plates.

Judge Carson met him when the ship finally docked at
Manila. The sight of the energetic boy made him realize
that it had been a serious blunder to invite Dick to the
troubled islands. In fact, Kit was to acquire many new
gray hairs before Dick finally departed.

On one occasion after Dick was ceremoniously made a
deputy sheriff in Sorsogon Province, he slipped away from
Kit on his wiry pony, El Diablo, and joined a posse round-
ing up ladrones, or bandits. He was gone three days and
barely escaped ambush. As he explained what happened:

> Suddenly, as I was approaching a small stream, sev-
> eral ladrones with bolos in their hands jumped out at
> me from the bush. They swept their heavy blades
> around and I whipped up my pony, heading for the
> river. They followed, but after I got through the water,
> they never had a chance to catch me. I never stopped
> until I found the detachment, where I was soundly
> scolded for my rashness.

When the opportunity presented itself to visit Darim Island, Kit let Dick go, but only after exacting a promise that Dick would stay out of trouble. However, unknown to Judge Carson, a cholera epidemic was sweeping that island. "Soon after I arrived," Dick reported later, "a soldier came in with pains in his stomach. With a professional air, I felt the man's pulse and declared him sick. The poor fellow died a few hours later."

Since Dick had been exposed to the soldier's cholera, he was quarantined with the Army garrison on top a hill. With his imaginative mind he developed several false symptoms of the dreaded disease. For several days he feared he would never see his family again. Yet while men died all about him, he remained free of the scourge. At Christmas time, with food supplies low, he was forced to make a dinner of parrots and monkeys. Finally, he smuggled out on a small boat and reached a port where he caught a ship back to Manila.

Even when he stayed close to Judge Carson, he managed to get into mischief. Because of the stifling heat and the sea of flies in his court, Judge Carson employed a breeze maker. A man hidden from view pulled cords attached to punkahs, or large palm-leaf fans. One day Dick talked the punkah puller into permitting him to try his hand at this task. However, Dick pulled so hard that the plaster came loose from the ceiling and dropped like a bomb on Kit. As a result, Kit hauled Dick before the bar and fined him all the money he had in his pockets.

Fearing that Dick might eventually contract cholera or be captured by ladrones, Judge Carson ended the visit at the end of April, 1903. During his few months in the

Philippines, the boy had had more adventures than perhaps a half-dozen soldiers. When it came time for Dick
to depart, Kit scheduled him to return home by the same
route he had come. "But I want to go home by a different
direction," Dick pleaded. "If I go home in the opposite
direction, then I will have gone clean around the world."

With a smile, Judge Carson agreed and Dick boarded
a British tramp steamer, the *Stratford*. He carried with him
the mark of an experienced adventurer, a large green par-
rot in a bamboo cage. Through the Indian Ocean, the
Suez Canal, the Mediterranean Sea and across the Atlantic
Dick came, unaware that many of his letters home had
been reprinted in newspapers. When his ship dropped
anchor at New York on July 4, he was surprised to find
twenty reporters clamoring for an interview with him.

He was only fourteen, and yet he was already known
for his travels!

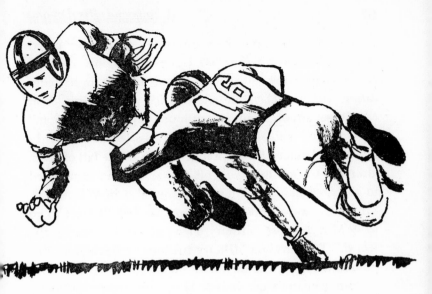

Chapter 2

AN EXPLORER'S EDUCATION

THE world of 1903 was a busy scene. So many events were taking place that the adventures of a fourteen-year-old boy were soon crowded off the front pages. Almost every day the colorful personality of President Theodore Roosevelt added zest to life in the United States. Almost every week, it seemed, Thomas Edison announced a new invention. That December the Wright brothers became the first to fly a heavier-than-air contraption.

In Winchester, Virginia, that year, Dick was impatient

to embark on bold new adventures. His wise father noted this and decided the time had come to bring his son back to everyday living. "We must attend to your formal education without delay," he said to Dick with finality. "You cannot get anywhere in life without a proper foundation."

Dick's first schooling had come at Miss Jennie Sherrard's school on Amherst Street in town. Then in the fall of 1898, after Kit Carson had gone off to war, he had transferred to the Shenandoah Valley Academy, also in Winchester. "If I must go to school," Dick now replied, "I want to go to V.M.I. because military men go everywhere in the world." The Virginia Military Institute at Lexington, Virginia, was reputed to be almost on a par with West Point.

"But you can't get into V.M.I.," his father sputtered. "They have a firm rule barring anyone under sixteen."

Nevertheless, at Dick's insistence, the elder Byrd made application at V.M.I. As was expected, the school's authorities sternly pointed to their minimum age rule. However, they did not count on the boy's persistence. In the end, exhausted, they agreed to make an exception on the ground of his excellence in mathematics, geography, and physics.

As Dick was to find, however, there was good reason for the rule. Besides being the youngest cadet, he was also the smallest. The older boys held him up as an object of ridicule and bullies busily tormented him at first. But later on he fortunately grew suddenly and became adept at protecting himself. By the time his third year began he was recognized as one of the outstanding members of his class.

However, he did not graduate from V.M.I. In 1907, at

the strong urging of his father, he transferred to the University of Virginia. His action brought on family talk that he would follow his father's footsteps and become a lawyer. But as the year crawled onward, his father became aware of Dick's growing unhappiness. If a boy were pushed into an unchosen field, the chances were he would lead an unhappy adult life.

In the spring of 1908, the elder Byrd asked his son to drop in and visit him at his law office. As soon as he entered, Dick knew something special was in the air because of the sparkle in his father's eyes. "Dick," said his father, "there's an opening for a Virginia lad at the Naval Academy. How would you like to take the exams and physical test?"

Dick could hardly reply. At nineteen now, he had almost given up his boyhood dream of manhood adventure and exploration. "Yes," he said weakly.

Only a short time later, Dick took the required examinations. And on May 28, 1908, he became a midshipman at the Naval Academy.

Here he lost no time in establishing himself as his class leader. Not only was he chairman of his plebe class but he managed to hold more offices than anyone else before he graduated in 1912. In addition, he poured his energies wholesale into almost every athletic program. Fellow classmen jokingly searched for sports in which he did not engage. This was difficult, for he went out for football, boxing, wrestling, track, tennis, gymnastics, and the rifle team. School records revealed that he was not merely a member of the various squads. He was wrestling champion for his weight, doubles tennis champion, captain and star of the gym team, and football quarterback, even though he weighed only 135 pounds. Though he did not go out for the swimming team, he managed to save a classmate from drowning in the Chesapeake.

Of course, a schedule of these dimensions affected his studies. Only in geography and navigation, applied physics and math, and in mechanical design, where he had strong natural aptitudes, did he excel. His language professors were convinced he should not travel abroad. "What are you going to do in France with your atrocious French accent?" one professor scolded him.

"They'll have to talk English to me," Dick grinned.

A good athlete must be alert. Yet off the athletic field Dick was known as a daydreamer. Once he faced a wrathful Commandant of Midshipmen whom he had neglected to salute. "I didn't see you," he apologized.

"But you walked right by me," the other chided him.

Another time military formation was called. When all the men were in place and awaiting inspection, Dick was discovered to be wearing bright yellow shoes instead of the required black. But this shortcoming was accepted as part of his make-up and no punishment was meted out to him.

The tendency at the Naval Academy at that time was to instill in the men the notion that they were a superior group. However, snobbery was entirely foreign to Dick. So far as he was concerned, everyone merited equal treatment. This issue came to a head when Dick served as chairman of the important Hop Committee.

One of the tasks of the committee was to issue invitations. Word reached Dick that the father of one midshipman had not been sent his invitation. "What is the reason for this?" he demanded of his fellow committeemen.

The others quickly pointed out that the boy's father was only a warrant officer in the Navy. It would not be proper to have him mingling socially with officers.

Dick grew furious at this lack of courtesy. "You can all go jump in the Severn River," he shouted.

Not only did he send the man an invitation, but he also made certain that he was treated well at the function.

No one dared contradict Dick because he was known as the class protector. A bully in Annapolis took great pleasure in administering physical beatings to midshipmen. There came a time when the men feared going singly into town. Finally an angry meeting of Dick's class elected him to meet this young man behind the hospital as class representative. Undaunted, Dick agreed, and there in the presence of a large crowd he and the larger bully punched each other for hours. When the morning ended, the bully asked for mercy and Dick was declared the winner though he was badly bruised and suffered a broken thumb. Characteristically, Dick later sought out his opponent and they became good friends.

At the Academy, Dick was also known as "Hard Luck Dick" because of his frequent physical mishaps. For instance, football was then a wide-open game and Dick was classified among the most reckless tacklers and ball carriers. Every week the sight of this wiry, curly-haired quarterback drew loud responses from the crowds, though many wondered how long he could compete against heavier players.

During his third year Navy played Princeton. The contest was rough and on one thrilling play Dick eluded tacklers to score a touchdown. Unfortunately, when he was already past the goal line, the Princeton team piled on him. When the whistle-blowing umpire pulled them off finally, Dick's right foot was broken in three places. If this was not enough, shortly after his recovery he contracted typhoid fever while on a training cruise. This laid him up for several months in an English hospital.

His worst accident occurred during his senior year. Believing that only a spectacular stunt would defeat the Yale gym team, he thought up a hair-raising trick on the flying rings. This involved a double somersault high off the floor and finally catching a swinging ring. One day, when the gym was filled with spectators to watch him practice his stunt, he went through his double somersault but failed to catch the flying ring. The audience let out a "queer sharp sigh" as he fell down.

His right ankle was smashed and doctors feared he would never walk again. A bony knot appeared on the outside of the ankle and clicked when he tried to walk. In the meantime he missed his semiannual exams and Academy officials advised him to drop back a class because he had fallen too far behind to prepare adequately for his final exams.

This he refused to do, even though little time remained after he finally left the hospital. After long hard nights of studying he limped to exam rooms and passed his final tests on schedule. He graduated only sixty-third in a class of 165, but considering his many activities and his foolish escapade on the flying rings this was a real achievement.

He always remembered his experience on the flying

rings as one of the important lessons in his life. "I learned this, at least, never to take myself too seriously and attach undue importance to my place in the scheme of things."

When he graduated in June, 1912, the opinion of his class was well summarized in the college yearbook. He was called "Athlete, leader in all right things, friend, gentleman. . . . He will always give to life more than he asks."

Chapter 3

AN ENSIGN IN THE NAVY

B Y THE time Byrd graduated from the Naval Academy,
important explorations had taken place at both ex-
tremes of the earth. On April 6, 1909, Robert E. Peary had
trudged across the frozen Arctic Ocean to that imaginary
point known as the Geographic North Pole. Then in December of 1911, an intrepid Norseman named Roald

Amundsen and his crew dashed by dog team across the ice continent of Antarctica to the South Pole. A month later Captain Robert F. Scott of England and his party duplicated Amundsen's feat only to perish on their return trip to their base.

If young Byrd felt the pangs of jealousy at these heroic feats, it was that he himself had hoped to be the first to accomplish them. But he knew there were other "firsts" left to mankind, and when the time came he hoped to achieve them.

In the meantime, he would train himself thoroughly for the opportunities that lay ahead.

It would be foolish to say that as a young ensign, Byrd's experiences differed from those of other beginning officers. There was much to learn about the navigation of a large man-of-war, the operation and firing of guns, and the maintenance of electrical and mechanical equipment. Yet in one important respect he did differ from his fellows: Adventure stalked him everywhere.

In 1914, stationed on a battleship, he found himself in the midst of military action to occupy Vera Cruz, Mexico. The Mexican dictator, Victoriano Huerta, had conducted a bitter anti-American campaign. This included trespassing on American property and arresting citizens of the United States. Byrd's battleship was part of the military force sent to capture the key Mexican city and thus drive Huerta from power.

Later, in the Caribbean zone, Byrd participated in actions to put down revolutions in San Domingo and Haiti. Whenever a landing party was needed, he was first to volunteer, and he walked miraculously through heavy gun-

fire without ever being wounded. He was also on ships
that were caught in violent storms and twice he saved
sailors from drowning. For instance, a captain reported
that after a sailor had been swept overboard into shark-
infested waters on August 15, 1914: "Byrd had made his
decision, and had dived from the high rail of the transport
without waiting to remove a single article of clothing.
Byrd made the line fast to the seaman," the captain went
on, "and insisted that the latter be rescued first. Meanwhile he remained in the rough water, still clad in his
soaked clothing, in constant danger of being dashed against
the ship's side, and a prey to the sudden attack of any lurking shark. Not until the man was safe aboard did Byrd consent to have himself hauled aboard." For this act of
heroism, he later won a Congressional life-saving medal
of honor.

Another distinguishing feature of Byrd's early years in
the Navy was that he possessed a remarkable hold over
enlisted men. He had the ability to put himself in their
place, and they recognized this. For instance, on the battleship *Washington* the crew consisted of recruits released
from naval prisons. Though several officers doubted the
wisdom of placing such persons under the charge of a new
ensign, Byrd proved more than able. Not only did the
men assigned to him work hard and willingly, but they
idolized their young superior.

There were other instances of the affection enlisted men
held for Byrd. Aboard the battleship *Wyoming,* he was assigned to serve as prosecuting officer in the trials of sailors.
Many an officer of the court considered with exasperation
his sympathy for defendants and his frequent appeals that

they be given another chance. When he considered sentences too harsh he worked strenuously to have them lightened.

Byrd's life was geared to warship existence until a chance event in late 1914 opened an entirely new world for him. Strolling on shore one day, he met a Navy captain who engaged him in conversation. "Say," said the captain after a while, "how would you like to ride in an airplane?"

Only eleven years before, the Wright brothers had made their historic first flight at Kitty Hawk, and airplanes had not progressed since then beyond a simple engine, wooden wings, wire struts, and open-air passenger seats. Without a moment of delay, Byrd took him up on the offer.

"I was right out in the open," Byrd described that first flight. "The plane had no fuselage. We sat on little seats and looked straight down, with nothing between us and the water. It was a great thrill."

Actually, it was more than a thrilling adventure. As the old seaplane wheezed aloft, a new determination passed through Byrd's mind. Perfected somewhat, the airplane could become an awesome machine. It would change the transportation means of the world. What was then a long trip to test the physical stamina of travelers could become a short and pleasant trip by air. There was also another factor of prime interest to him. An explorer like brave Peary was in a sense similar to a horse with blinders. He saw only the small tortured route that he fought along on his way to his goal. He did not see what lay even five or ten miles on either side of him. By airplane an explorer would be able to take in a vast panorama covering dozens of miles at a time.

Excitedly, he wrote home about his flight and announced his intention of becoming a pilot.

"Keep your feet on the ground," his worried father wrote back by return mail.

Though he wanted badly to fly, as an ensign Byrd was at the bottom of the officer totem pole and had little to say about where he wished to serve. In fact, shortly after he expressed his desire to leave ships for airplanes, an order came for him to report to Washington, D.C. It was the style then to assign obscure but handsome, dashing young officers to Washington duty to help fill the needs of the social season there.

Byrd soon found himself languishing aboard the *Dolphin,* the official yacht of Secretary of the Navy Josephus Daniels. Instead of excitement, there were only quiet weekend cruises down the Potomac and a social existence the rest of the time. If there was a single saving feature of this period, it was the warm friendship that developed between Byrd and the young Assistant Secretary of the Navy. This was thirty-two-year-old Franklin D. Roosevelt who was one day destined to become President. Roosevelt revealed an enormous interest in ships and the Navy, and he and Byrd cemented a close personal relationship that was to last until Roosevelt's death.

Byrd's Washington stay was also made more pleasant by the fact that he married his childhood sweetheart during this period. She was pretty Marie Ames and they were married on January 20, 1915. Byrd's two brothers, Harry and Tom, served jointly as "best man" at the ceremony.

Shortly after his marriage, Byrd was notified that he was to leave the *Dolphin* and shift to the *Mayflower* in the same harbor. This was scant improvement in fulfilling his general desires, though it proved a vital experience. For the *Mayflower* was the official yacht of President Woodrow Wilson.

Often on the many weekend cruises down the Potomac and into the Chesapeake, Byrd had ample opportunity to observe the President in meetings with other government officials. Occasionally the President engaged him in conversation and reminisced about his days at the University of Virginia with Byrd's father. At other times he spoke of the national and world scenes and broadly enlarged the outlook of his young listener.

So life moved along at this amiable pace until tragedy struck. Aboard the Battleship *Wyoming* a few years earlier, Byrd's bad ankle had collapsed and he had fallen down a steep gangway. On that occasion, he had gone to the hospital for three months. There doctors had pounded an ordinary galvanized nail through the weakened ankle to hold the separated bones together.

The leg had given him no real trouble since then. But now aboard the *Mayflower* he found it painful to stand long hours on watch duty. It was his poor luck also that at the height of his discomfort he was notified to report for his annual routine medical examination in March of 1916.

The doctors were quick to notice his swollen ankle. "Your ankle has not healed properly," they told him.

"But it will," he replied.

The chief examiner shook his head. "Our decision is

that you can no longer remain on active duty. I'm afraid we shall have to retire you."

The words were like a bombshell exploding. "But don't worry." The doctor patted his shoulder. "Even though you will be retired, you will be raised from ensign to lieutenant junior grade on the retired list." He smiled at Byrd. "Just think, you'll be able to draw three-quarters of your pay at that higher rate the rest of your life."

Marie Byrd read the black despair on her husband's face when he returned home. There was no appeal from the medical board's decision, he told her. At twenty-eight his active naval career was at an end—and so were his dreams. "Five futile years," he blurted. "Not enough income to live on. Not a chance of coming back. It's the end of everything."

Chapter 4

PIONEER IN AVIATION

IN ordinary times, Byrd's naval career would have been at an end and he would have been forced to seek some civilian pursuit. However, 1916 was not an ordinary year.

In faraway Europe, World War I neared the close of its second grim year. Beleaguered Germany had begun to molest the ships of the United States, which was not in the war. Stung by this disregard for the traditional freedom

of the seas, President Wilson ordered a national program
of military preparedness.

As a result, Byrd's retirement lasted only two months.
In May, while he was still trying to decide what civilian
job to accept, the Navy requested him to proceed to Rhode
Island. There he was to undertake the reorganization of
the state's naval militia. This was a volunteer force within
the state whose morale had vanished and whose men were
resigning.

Byrd leaped at this opportunity to return to the Navy's
active list and lost no time in stamping his strong personality upon the Rhode Island militia. Though the men
who preceded him considered his task hopeless, he quickly
restored morale, devised an excellent training program
and was soon flooded with a long list of applicants. To
learn more about the business aspects of organization,
Byrd sped each day to classes at Harvard and then returned
to apply what he had learned.

Several months after he undertook this job, he announced that his mission was successful. So enthusiastic
was the Governor of Rhode Island that he wrote to the
Navy Department:

> I ascribe most of the credit of this to Commander
> Byrd, for whom I predict a brilliant career, if only the
> opportunity for service can be given him.

It was Byrd's hope that the Navy would now give him
the opportunity to return to sea duty. But this was not to
be because Navy records listed him as "crippled." Instead
he was ordered to report to Washington to a desk job,

where, as he put it, his job was to transfer "enlisted men from station to station, and official papers from basket to basket."

The days on end that he had to spend indoors made him unhappy. But there was nothing he could do about the situation. Noting his condition, Navy Secretary Daniels called him in one day and transferred him to a much more important desk job. This was an assignment to serve as executive secretary of the Navy Commission on Training Camps.

This was no small task, for the function of the commission was to improve the health and education of sailors who were now swarming into the service. Most of those who served with Byrd found the assignment challenging. For instance, his close friend Walter Camp, who had modernized football rules and now handled the athletic program, thought up a series of exercises that he named the "Daily Dozen."

But to Byrd the job meant only "a bigger desk and deeper baskets." For in April of 1917, the United States declared war on Germany and he wanted to get into the fighting. "I lost twenty-five pounds worrying over the uselessness of what I had become—just a high-class clerk," he said.

His frequent pleas for active duty finally brought him before the medical examining board. But this time the doctors were not even convinced he should keep his swivel-chair job. "You'll have to take leave, Byrd," the head doctor told him bluntly. "You are in terrible condition."

The shock of this remark almost overwhelmed Byrd. "Give me a chance," he blurted. "I want to fly. Give me a month of it and if I don't improve to suit you, I'll get out without another word."

"But we can't give you active duty with that leg." The chief examiner shook his head.

"But you don't fly with your legs," Byrd pleaded.

The doctors smiled. It was true that flying did not include long hours of standing watch. "All right," they said reluctantly in the end. "You can have a month to prove yourself. After a month at flying school, you will have to take another physical exam, and we'll reserve final judgment until then."

This was truly the turning point in Byrd's life, for at last he was being given the opportunity he had long sought. However, at the time the circumstances did not seem right because he was ill and underweight and almost at the point of a breakdown. Moreover, his father was crushed by the news that he was to begin training as a flier. "When I entered aviation," said Byrd, "my father told me goodbye. It was his impression that he would never see me alive again."

With a certain amount of sadness mingled with his joy, Byrd reported to the Naval Training Station at Pensacola, Florida, in August, 1917. This sadness was increased as he came across the beach with his suitcase clutched in his hand. High in the sky a plane maneuvered. Suddenly, while Byrd watched it, the plane came plummeting down to an exploding crash in the bay. Byrd's mouth went dry and his shoulders hunched when he learned that its two occupants were dead.

"Does this happen often?" he asked an officer in horror.

"Oh, every day," was the casual reply. "Sometimes two or three times a day."

Byrd gulped when within the hour he was asked to go up for his first lesson. "I never felt less like flying in my entire life," he said. Nevertheless, he put on his flying uniform and went aloft.

What the officer told him was true. The planes were wobbly and unstable craft and the men were ordered to solo before they were ready. The men had a silent understanding that many would never leave Pensacola alive.

In Byrd's case, he was told he was ready to solo after only six hours of instruction. Inwardly he felt he was born to fly and gave not a thought to his lack of experience. "Twenty minutes' flying is enough," his instructor warned him after shaking hands. While Byrd's seaplane was being pushed into the water, he looked back and saw an expression of doom on his instructor's ashen face.

Byrd's take-off was smooth and soon he was in the air. "First flight alone is probably the greatest event in a pilot's life," he said afterward. "Never again does a flier feel the same thrill."

He had no trouble so long as he stayed in the air. However, coming down for a landing, he hit the water with a loud splash. Luckily, his plane bounced back into the air. He could see his instructor with a hand over his eyes. For an hour and twenty minutes, Byrd tried landings. Finally he came down smoothly and taxied in proudly. He was now a flier.

As the days passed, his pale face grew tan and he took on weight. The fresh air and physical activity increased his appetite, and the love of flying gave zest to his life. Not

satisfied with being anything less than the best, he prac-
ticed hundreds of landings. He also took engines apart
and studied the pieces as they lay on greasy cloths. Then
he reassembled the engines bolt by bolt and later flew
planes where they were installed. It was little wonder that
he passed his next physical with flying colors.

Shortly after winning his wings, Byrd progressed to the
rank of instructor. He was also named Assistant Superin-
tendent at Pensacola, and took on still other assignments.
One of these was to learn and teach the art of night flying.
This meant taking off and landing in the dark, a rather
difficult task that called for strong nerves and great skill.
On Byrd's first blind flight he narrowly averted disaster.
But he went on to become an expert at this art and trained
the first naval squadron of night fighters.

Byrd also served as a member of the Crash Board at
Pensacola. It was the task of this group to investigate plane
crashes and to determine what could be done to make flying safer. Unfortunately, the Crash Board was able to find
reasons for crashes but seldom could offer preventive solu-
tions for the future. For instance, no one then knew how
to get out of a tail spin. Also, there were no traffic rules
in the skies and air collisions were common. That airplanes could be treated like automobiles never crossed
anyone's mind.

Because of the great number of accidents at Pensacola,
the Crash Board had plenty of work. Even Byrd, who by
now was cautioning all fliers to fly carefully, was not himself immune. On one occasion, his plane had just left the
water and was plowing upward at sixty miles an hour
when another plane came down from the sky and headed

toward him. "The crash was deafening," said Byrd. "We were just enough out of line to make our wings lock. . . . Both planes were demolished." By a miracle of fate, both Byrd and the other pilot were hauled from the water with only bruises to show for their near tragedy.

Early in 1918, Byrd conceived a bold plan to fly across the Atlantic Ocean. No one in history had done this and Byrd proposed to be the first. He had learned that the Navy had begun building the three-motored NC-1, the largest flying boat in the world, with an expected cruising range far in excess of any other plane so far developed. He wrote in May to his friend Walter Camp of his desire and outlined his plan. He would deliver the plane to the Allied Commander in Chief in Europe after a refueling stop in the Azores. The flight, he believed, would serve to lower German morale. An important additional value of the flight, he considered, was the knowledge to be gained about ocean flying, then entirely a mystery.

Shortly afterward, Byrd learned that Camp and Admiral Peary of North Pole fame had urged Navy officials to approve such a flight. On July 9, when he learned that the NC-1 was nearing completion, Byrd formally made his request to the Navy.

It has been my ambition to make such a flight [he wrote]. I feel that I am well qualified to be given this detail, in that I have made an intensive study of the subject, have specialized in air navigation and am thoroughly familiar with the larger type of flying boat.

For two weeks Byrd waited impatiently for a reply. Then came a telegram ordering him to Washington. Cheers rang out at Pensacola when word spread regarding Byrd's good fortune. The men hurried to his room to press his hand and pat his back. "You're the luckiest man alive," they congratulated him, and Byrd agreed.

He left Pensacola in such haste that he overlooked several valuable personal belongings. But what was the difference? he consoled himself. As his train sped northward, he said to himself, "I ought to be on my way across in the NC-1 by October first at the very latest."

The capital sweltered in its most humid weather of the year when he arrived. Quickly he made his way through the crowded city to the Navy Department. The oppressive heat meant nothing to him as he bounded into the building to learn the details of the plans the Navy had for him and the large NC-1.

Unfortunately, he could find no one who would confirm his imminent flight. At the same time no one would say that he had been called to Washington for any other reason. Days passed in this fashion as he trudged from one official to another.

Then on August 12, he was finally given sealed orders. No mention was made of the Atlantic flight. Instead, he was ordered to proceed immediately to Halifax, Nova Scotia. He was to become Commanding Officer of the U. S. Air Force in Canada.

"But I don't want to be shunted off to Canada," he said as he burst into offices of influential Navy officials. "I want to fly the Atlantic."

"You will do as you are ordered," was the standard reply.

Crestfallen, Byrd gave up for the time being his most earnest desire.

Chapter 5

AN AMERICAN ABROAD

ONE of Byrd's chief characteristics was that he never permitted personal ambitions to rule over his loyalty to the Navy. For instance, once he received orders to proceed to Canada, he plunged wholeheartedly into the task.

In this case, the task was no small matter. Because of the huge increase in freight traffic, wartime railroads were badly overburdened. Byrd found that he had to argue for

days before he could put his planes and equipment on
trains bound for Halifax. And once he arrived in Canada, he learned that the Canadian Government had given
him a piece of land on a rough coast eight miles across the
bay from Halifax. This meant that he had to float his
planes and gear across the turbulent water. Arriving at his
base, he and his crew had no trucks to haul supplies and
had to do so by hand. They also lacked regular boards and
were forced to construct their camp from scrap-packaging
pieces of lumber. All these hindrances meant round-the-
clock labor with Byrd setting the pace personally at the
dozens of jobs. Nevertheless, only three short days after
beginning work, the base was in operation.

Byrd worked his pilots hard, for their responsibility
was to keep enemy submarines clear of the coast. Until
then, German subs had had a field day destroying dozens
of ships in the northwestern Atlantic. He taught his men
how to bank and turn their planes properly. He also in-
structed them in the new art of parachute jumping. The
system he used was to have his jumpers go up in balloons
to a height of 1,000 feet and then leap from the under-
hanging baskets of the balloons. He was never able to
overcome his tenseness "when a black form shot downward
dragging with it what looked like a streamer of rag."

In patrolling the coastal area, Byrd and his men often
had to fly over water and out of sight of land. Once in this
position, fliers had to depend often on instinct to get them
back safely to shore. To remedy this situation Byrd in-
vented a "bubble" sextant. With this instrument, fliers
were able to locate their position by taking altitudes of
the sun.

During that summer of 1918 only a single submarine was reported close to Halifax Harbor. Putting his training to good use, Byrd went after it himself. However, when he came down low over what looked like the submarine's periscope, he found it to be merely a vertical floating spar that had come loose from a ship.

Although he put in long days with his flying squadron, Byrd also busied himself with two other activities. Never having been told officially that the transatlantic flight had been discarded, he spent off hours studying routes across the Atlantic, oceanic navigation problems, and determining what instruments, food and clothing would be required. In addition, he bombarded Washington with letters until he won the promise that soon he would be sent to the fighting front in Europe.

However, the Armistice was declared on November 11, 1918, and he was ordered to turn over his command to Canadian officers and return to Washington. "I felt I hadn't done my share," he said. In addition, he believed that his big "plan for a transatlantic flight had evaporated" because "the attendant risk would not be permitted now that peace had come."

As Byrd dwelt on his disappointment, the words of Admiral Peary came to his mind. "Fortunately I did not know that Fate was even then clenching her fist for still another crushing blow." This, too, was to happen to Byrd.

On his way to Washington, he learned that the Navy had not dropped its plan to stage a transatlantic flight. In fact, the schedule called for the earliest possible take-off. Wild with excitement, he rushed from Union Station to

the Navy Department in Washington. He tried to main-
tain his calm: "Well, here I am."

Two orders were handed him. The first said that Commander John H. Towers was to be "placed in command
of the Trans-Atlantic flight which is to go through at
once." Byrd felt like shouting with joy that the flight was
confirmed. What difference did it make who was in charge
so long as he would be on the plane?

Then he read the second report and his dreams disinte-
grated. It said:

> No officer or man who has had foreign duty will be
> permitted to be a member of the Trans-Atlantic flight
> expedition. This includes those who have been on
> Canadian detail.

Nor was the harshness of this blow eased by a further
order sending Byrd back to Pensacola, Florida.

Disheartened, Byrd fell ill with influenza, which had
overtaken thousands in Washington. As he lay in bed, he
tried to think of reasons why he had to take part in the
ocean expedition. Certainly no man knew more than he
about flying over water. Staggering down a hospital corri-
dor, he put in a phone call to Commander Towers. "Do
you still want me to help out on the flight?" he asked
weakly.

"Decidedly so," said Towers.

Sick as he was, Byrd sought out the Navy captain who
had assigned him to Pensacola. Listening to the pale young
man argue, the captain decided to be merciful. "You can
help Towers in the preliminary work," he said. "But

under no circumstances can you go along on the flight."
On wobbly legs, Byrd thanked him.

It was as an expert in flight and navigation problems
that Byrd joined the Navy's Trans-Atlantic Flight Section.
By the spring of 1919 he learned that the Navy planned
to send not only the NC-1 but also her two sisters, the
NC-3 and NC-4. Each plane had an upper wingspread of
126 feet and a fuselage length of 63 feet. With a cruising
speed of 75 miles an hour, each plane was expected to travel
about 1,500 miles nonstop. Because the ocean was wider
than this, the planes would fly to Europe in steps: first to
Halifax, Nova Scotia; then to Trepassey, Newfoundland;
next to Horta in the Azores; and finally to Portugal.

As chief navigation officer for the trio of planes, Byrd
was faced with many complex problems. For instance, a
strong wind could easily blow a plane so far off course that
a pilot might lose his bearings. The Navy proposed sta-
tioning warships every fifty miles along the route to Europe. However, Byrd objected on the ground that while
this would help the pilots something more permanent was
necessary. To solve the problem, Byrd developed a drift
indicator that told the pilot how much he had to alter his
course to correct for the wind.

There were several mishaps before the planes were
ready to quit their home base at Rockaway, on Long Island. Propellers cracked, tanks leaked, and men were
maimed. On one occasion just after Byrd landed from a
trial flight aboard the NC-4, the rudder wires collapsed.
Had this occurred only a minute before, the plane would
have collapsed in mid-air.

On May 8, 1919, the three planes took off for the nine-hour trip to Halifax. "Come along with me on the NC-3 as far as Trepassey," Towers invited Byrd. Later Towers described the first leg of the Atlantic flight:

> Byrd spent the afternoon vibrating between the forward and after cockpits, trying smoke bombs, sextants, etc. My cockpit was not very large, and with all the charts, chart desk, sextants, drift indicator, binoculars, chronometers, etc., stacked in there, very little room was left. As I wore a telephone all the time, wires were trailing all about me, and Byrd and I were continually getting all mixed up like a couple of puppies on leashes.

When the plane came down at stop number two at Trepassey, Newfoundland, Washington was now far away. Byrd hoped that the Navy would take no notice if he completed the flight across the ocean. Towers was not opposed to this. But shortly after the landing, telegraphic orders came bluntly telling Byrd to leave the detail. To soften the blow, however, the Navy ordered him to report for duty to the small Navy dirigible, the C-5, that was stationed nearby at St. John's, Newfoundland.

"There's your chance, Dick, to cross the ocean after all," said Towers. Byrd knew that there had been some talk of flying the C-5 across the Atlantic. "You can drift over, if you don't do anything else," Towers added.

"If I got away and aboard her," Byrd wrote later, "and she flew, there was still a chance that the miracle for which I hoped might happen."

But his high tide of bad luck was still running strong. The very next day came the following radio message: "The C-5 has broken loose from her moorings in a storm and blown away with no personnel aboard her." His last flickering hope was now extinguished.

On May 16, he assisted in the departure of the planes for Europe. Then he trudged up a high hill and watched them take off. He shook his head jealously as they disappeared over the ocean.

Neither the NC-1 nor the NC-3 reached Europe. Both planes crash-landed in the ocean, though all crew members were rescued. However, the NC-4 under Lt. Com. A. C. Read reached Horta in the Azores after fifteen hours in the air. Then after a wait of several days, a ten-hour flight brought the plane safely to Portugal. For the first time in history a plane had spanned the Atlantic Ocean.

"Why not get out of flying?" his brother Tom counseled him when he returned to Washington. Tom had amassed a superb war record and was now a lawyer and apple grower in Virginia. "You are thirty-one now, Dick. Try something less dangerous for a change."

Byrd would not take his advice. He realized that aviation was still considered a toy by most of the admirals in the Navy. More than ever he wanted to win an honored place for the airplane as a vital defense tool.

To gain status for the airplane, he wrote a bill creating a Bureau of Aeronautics in the Navy. Though the admirals opposed this, he took his bill to Navy Secretary Daniels. "Now what are you going to do?" asked the kindly North Carolinian.

"Get Congress to pass the bill."

Daniels thought awhile and then he smiled. "Let me write a strong letter of endorsement for you," he said finally.

Byrd took his bill to the Capitol. Though he knew little about Congress and the way a bill became law, he soon became an expert. One Senator agreed to sponsor the bill in the Senate; a Representative took on the same job in the House. There were many tense moments in committee hearings and in floor debate. But in the end, after Byrd had sold himself and his cause to dozens of Congressmen, his bill became law. The Bureau of Aeronautics took its place as an important part of the Navy.

Throughout his long career following this success, the Navy often called upon Byrd for help to get vital legislation through Congress.

It was Byrd's opinion that after his work on the bill the Navy owed him a small favor, and he asked permission to fly alone across the Atlantic. He proposed to fly 1,909 miles nonstop from Newfoundland to England. "What!" exclaimed Assistant Secretary Theodore Roosevelt, Jr. "Everyone knows that airplane engines are not reliable on long flights. Besides, Byrd is too valuable to lose."

Instead, the Navy proposed that Byrd go to England by boat and help navigate the new ZR-2 dirigible on its nonstop flight to the United States. This was not what Byrd had requested, but he quickly agreed to this daring undertaking. The ZR-2 had been built in England for the American Navy. Measuring 700 feet in length with a diameter of 85 feet, she was the largest dirigible in the world. A safe passage across the ocean would do much to advance dirigible travel.

Byrd arrived in London on August 20, 1921. Learning that the ZR-2 planned a trial flight the following day, he telephoned the field at Howden to reserve a seat on the airship. He was told that places were scarce but if he came in person, the British would find a seat for him.

Although he rushed to the train station, he missed the Howden train by a scant two minutes. The Byrd bad luck was still with him, he told himself. It was not until nighttime that he reached Howden and learned that no more seats were available. Since he had not come when he was expected, he was out in the cold. He would have to wait for the regular flight some time later across the ocean.

Byrd's last resort was to board the airship after it came out of the hangar and onto the field. He had heard that one of the mechanics was not actually needed for the flight and he asked if he could replace him. "But I've sent my whole family and baggage ahead to Pulham, sir, where we're going to tie up to the mooring mast," the mechanic protested. "It would make a mess of things for me if I don't go up in her."

"It was a mixed feeling that came over me as I watched the big shiny airship lift slowly into the air," said Byrd.

The ZR-2 was to cruise all that night. So Byrd took the train back to London for a later leisurely trip to Pulham. Early the following evening as he made his way to the London railroad station, he suddenly stopped walking. A newsboy was shouting, "Extry! Read all about the big airship crash!"

It was true, as Byrd discovered when he ripped a paper
from the newsboy's hands. The ZR-2 had exploded in mid-
air and had fallen like a torch into the Humber River near
Hull. Of her fifty men, there were only five survivors. The
two-minute margin by which he had missed the train to
Howden had saved Byrd's life.

Chapter 6

FLYING OVER THE NORTH POLE

IN October of 1921 when Byrd celebrated his thirty-third birthday, it was a good time to take stock of his path through life. Most of his friends were already well settled into their life's work, while he seemed to be getting nowhere. His early goals of pioneering and exploring appeared to be as far away as ever. Certainly he had achieved a degree of success in advancing the cause of aviation, but his own personal accomplishments were meager.

Yet he did not feel sorry for himself. One day, he believed, his bad luck would be swept away by a wide broom and in its place his dreams would rise. As he put it: "If one sticks at it hard enough and long enough he will at last find the key to the door of success."

One of his first acts to put his house in order was to request the Navy to place him on inactive duty. As a peacetime measure his temporary rank was to be lowered from lieutenant commander to lieutenant. With a growing family he could not well exist on this demoted salary. In addition, he believed he might do better at air expeditions if he did not have the Navy constantly overriding his plans.

However, the Navy had important bills before Congress. Byrd was an expert in dealing with legislators, so why let him go? The result was that Byrd was requested to remain until the bills passed Congress. Like the loyal naval officer that he was, Byrd agreed to this temporary arrangement.

It was while he was buttonholing Congressmen on these bills that he conceived the idea of having the Navy establish peacetime aviation reserve stations across the country. Not only would these serve as refresher bases for experienced war fliers but they would also be a means to attract young men into the field. So excited did Byrd become with his plans that for the time being he laid aside his desire to enter civilian life.

Unfortunately, Congress adjourned before he could make much headway. Nevertheless, he broached the subject to top Navy officials. "Your plan is excellent," they told him, "but we haven't any money to put it into existence. What would you suggest?"

"I would build Navy air stations without money," Byrd replied.

"All right, you do it," came the skeptical retort.

Only a day later Byrd arrived at Squantum, Massachusetts, the proposed site of his first reserve air station. Quickly he put out an urgent emergency call to all former war fliers in the area. Then he organized voluntary work parties of sailors from nearby ships to help build runways and hangars. Lumber came from a junk pile and tools came from generous donors. Soon afterward Byrd and his men put together a rickety plane and began air instruction.

The response from the Navy was enthusiastic. Byrd had given birth to the Naval Reserve Air Force, and for his success he would have to remain a while longer in the Navy. Not only would he be called upon to establish other reserve air stations but he would also be asked to go before Congress and win money for their permanent operation.

During all this period, which ran through 1923, Byrd had had little time to think about his long-range plans. He was entirely out of the public eye except for one heroic deed. This occurred one night in January, 1922, when a heavy snowstorm blanketed Washington. As Byrd was riding out of the capital, a policeman suddenly stopped his car. "Turn around and take me to the Knickerbocker Theatre on Eighteenth Street!" the policeman screamed. "The theatre's caved in!"

Arriving on the scene after a wild drive through the storm, Byrd saw that the roof had collapsed from the weight of the snow. With a disregard for his own safety, he rushed into the twisted ruins to save trapped people.

Using all the muscles he had developed through weight lifting, he raised great timbers to free individuals caught in the debris. For four hours wherever he heard a human cry in the darkness, he blithely ignored the warnings of the police and went to the rescue.

A total of 98 persons died in the cave-in and many more would not have survived had it not been for Byrd. For his effort he was cited for extreme heroism: "His coolness, judgment and ability to group bystanders into actual working parties resulted in an early liberation for many wounded." Said another citation: "His entire conduct the night of this disaster was characterized by extraordinary heroism and superb conduct."

For his selfless efforts in promoting reserve air stations, the Navy decided to honor Byrd's great interest in exploration. In January, 1924, while he was in Chicago where he organized the air station at the Great Lakes Training Station, Byrd was ordered to report to Washington. "President Coolidge has approved our project to send our new dirigible, the *Shenandoah,* across the North Pole," naval officers explained to him. "We want you to help prepare the flight and also to go along."

If Byrd had told them that bad luck had plagued almost all his expected adventures, and that something would now also occur, they probably would have smiled. Nevertheless, only a few days later a severe storm ripped the *Shenandoah* from her mooring mast, pounded her helpless skeleton crew for eight miserable hours, and damaged the airship. Shortly afterward President Coolidge called off the projected polar flight.

But the idea of flying over the North Pole was too good

for Byrd to drop. He did not have to look far to find ample reasons why he should make the attempt. The large dream that he had hidden in the pages of his diary when he was twelve years old had become a lifelong desire. Second, it would add to the prestige of the United States to be the first to fly over the North Pole. Last but not least, an airplane trip across the Pole would do much to hasten public acceptance of the airplane.

To go on his quest for the unknown, Byrd now went on the Navy's retired list. Free from military responsibilities, he set out to win private backing for his proposed flight. First to join him was Captain Bob Bartlett, who had served as skipper of the *Roosevelt*, Peary's ship on his North Pole trip. Raising money was no simple task, for Byrd was embarrassed to come hat in hand for aid. In Detroit, he barged into the office of Edsel Ford, the son of Henry Ford, and came away with a promise of $15,000. John D. Rockefeller, Jr., assured him of a similar amount.

Even so, he did not raise sufficient funds to purchase airplanes. Fortunately, President Coolidge heard of his plight and offered him the use of two of the three military amphibian planes owned by the government.

Byrd was soon in the midst of intensive preparations. He had to acquire and test equipment, train men and lay careful plans so there would be no slip-up. As he often said later, "You have adventures on expeditions only because you planned your undertaking poorly."

An unforeseen problem arose. In the midst of his work, Byrd learned that Donald B. MacMillan planned an expedition on the southern and western sections of Greenland. It was Byrd's intention to set his base at the north-west tip of Greenland. From here he planned to conduct an air expedition over the 1,000,000 square miles of unknown area north of the Arctic Circle. He would also search for a supply and refueling base on land he hoped to find in the polar sea. Then from this advance base he would make his flight over the North Pole.

So far as he could see, there were no conflicting interests between him and MacMillan. Nevertheless, the Navy ruled that if Byrd were to acquire use of its amphibian planes, he must join forces with MacMillan. Furthermore, MacMillan would be in charge of the combined expedition.

This was an unhappy situation for Byrd, but he was in no position to complain. Quickly he gave his consent, and on June 20, 1925, the combined expedition departed from Maine aboard the *Peary* for the 3,000-mile voyage to Etah, North Greenland.

Etah means "windy place," and is the northernmost home of the Eskimos. With the help of the Smith Sound Eskimos there and his own crew of eight, Byrd built a runway for his planes of the crates that had guarded the wings of the planes on the voyage. The runway ran over the rocky beach which Byrd called "the best beach anywhere near Etah and one of the worst ones I've ever seen." Work proceeded fairly rapidly despite the cold because the sun was in the sky twenty-four hours each day.

From his long training, Byrd had learned the value of careful preparation. He had even brought along carrier pigeons so that if he were forced to land, the birds would fly back to Etah with that news. Unfortunately, when he released ten birds for a trial flight, six were killed almost immediately by huge arctic falcons.

There was one unforeseen failure. So little was known about that area that Byrd's estimate of the remaining summer's length was a poor guess. He had come so late that there were but fifteen days of summer remaining. And of the fifteen only three were good flying days.

Consequently, Byrd readily understood that he would have to make a second expedition if he were to fly over the North Pole. With his precious time fleeting, Byrd flew several reconnaissance flights to search out suitable landing places en route to the Pole. But in all the 30,000 square miles he and his other pilots surveyed the ice was so rough that planes could not land.

Although this expedition was not successful so far as Byrd's ambitions were concerned, it was highly useful. From it, Byrd amassed a great deal of personal information about the arctic region. This would help him immensely when he came again. He also learned that Etah was not the best jumping-off point for a flight across the North Pole. He would have to select a safer site.

However, the most important feature of his trip was that he made the acquaintance and became a close personal friend of an aviation mechanic named Floyd Bennett. Bennett was only an enlisted man in the Navy who had served aboard various men-of-war. Others who served with him did not consider him to be out of the ordinary. Yet Byrd both sensed and brought out his hidden qualities.

On the MacMillan Expedition, Floyd Bennett proved to be a superb pilot and fully as brave as Byrd. He had an uncanny sense of direction and could manipulate an airplane as if it were a toy. Like Byrd, he was born without fear. For instance, on one flight from Etah, the oil in the

tank heated dangerously. There was little question in
Byrd's mind that the tank would soon explode and destroy
their plane. Without a word, Bennett inched his way out
on the wing in the heavy storm and calmly unscrewed the
cap on the tank, thus relieving the pressure.

The most important flight Byrd and Bennett made on
this expedition was not northward toward the Pole. Instead, it was a flight to test the cruising range and high-
altitude capabilities of their plane. This was the first trip
made by man across the Greenland icecap, a solid ice sheet
more than a mile high. The plane performed so well that
when Byrd returned to Etah he was "stirred with the con-
clusion that aviation could conquer the Arctic."

When 1926 dawned, Byrd was not the only explorer
working to reach the North Pole. Captain George Wilkins
was already at Nome, Alaska, where he waited in readiness
for good weather with his planes and dogs. In Norway,
Captain Roald Amundsen, who had been first to reach
the South Pole, in December, 1911, was now preparing a
dirigible expedition over the North Pole. It would be a
race to see which of the three crossed the earth's northern
extreme first.

There were three available places Byrd could have
utilized as his work base for the flight. First, there was
Point Barrow, the northernmost point of Alaska. But Point
Barrow was actually far from the Pole. Furthermore, ships
could not penetrate that far until late summer because
of the solid ice. Flight was then too dangerous because the
polar sea would be coated with heavy fog.

Etah was a second possibility because it lay 400 miles
closer to the Pole than Point Barrow. But Byrd had

learned the previous year that Etah lacked a safe take-off strip for land planes. This left Spitsbergen as the best basing zone and Kings Bay there as the best base point, for it lay only 750 miles from the Pole. Warmed by the Gulf Stream, Kings Bay might be reached as early as April.

This time Byrd did not plan an expedition supported by the government. It would be a private expedition whose costs would have to be met by himself. Since he had no money, this meant asking others, a process he did not enjoy. Nevertheless, it was necessary, and he found he had many friends and supporters. He acquired a plane and he named this three-engine single-wing machine the *Josephine Ford,* after the three-year-old daughter of Edsel Ford, his chief supporter. He also acquired the temporary use of a small steamer, the *Chantier,* and a crew of forty-six, most of whom went along at no pay. Some businessmen gave him food; others gave oil, coal, clothing, and other supplies. For his other needs Byrd raised more than $100,-000. Even so, he left owing more than $20,000 which he hoped to repay by selling the story of his expedition to newspapers.

The *Chantier* left New York on April 25, 1926, far behind Byrd's schedule. When Byrd got to Kings Bay, Spitsbergen, on the 29th, he found the Amundsen crew already there and busily preparing for the arrival of the Italian airship, the *Norge.* Fast work was essential now.

However, from the outset there were several difficult problems. The *Chantier* could not anchor closer than 900 yards from shore because the harbor lay in a mass of jagged ice. This created a real puzzler—how to bring his airplane ashore. Byrd did not hesitate, lowering the four whaleboats carried by the *Chantier* into an open patch of water and laying heavy planks over the boats to make a raft. On this he lowered his large plane, and armed with oars his men tried to thread their way through the ice floes to shore. When an immense iceberg threatened to override the raft, Byrd blew it to bits with dynamite. "My relief was great," said Byrd, "when we at last reached the ice foot protruding from the beach." There lay ahead an even bigger task of pulling the plane a mile up a long hill to the landing site. But the men having come this far considered this a routine effort.

Byrd, Floyd Bennett, and the others averaged less than five hours' sleep each day as they hurried preparations for the flight. The hardest job was leveling the snow on the take-off field. Three sets of skis were broken in trial take-offs. Finally a durable set was constructed from boat oars.

Now came the test to rise from the ice into the air. However, the snow runway was still too bumpy and the skis clung to the snow as if magnetized. The plane finally passed the runway's end and plowed into a huge snowdrift. Neither Byrd nor Bennett was injured, though they were heartsick about possible damage to the plane. A broad smile crossed their faces later when they found the plane still in excellent shape.

On May ninth, the weatherman reported that the day was excellent for a flight. Byrd and Bennett had gone thirty-six hours without sleep, but they knew that they must take advantage of the weather. "It's now or never," said Bennett. "We'll either get the *Josephine Ford* off the ice or crash into oblivion." Some of the other men tried to dissuade them because they were too tired to go off on the 1,500-mile round trip. If they crashed en route, it would take them an estimated two years to make their way back—if they were lucky. They had only a ten-week food supply and they would have to kill seals and polar bears in order to survive. "Let's go," said Byrd.

The take-off was smooth. Once in the air, Byrd and Bennett took turns piloting the plane. They could not rely on the magnetic compass to steer them toward the Pole because the North Magnetic Pole which attracted the north compass position lay more than a thousand miles away from the true Pole at Boothia Peninsula, Canada. Instead they relied on a sun compass, which told direction by the shadow of the sun. Then to steer a true course, they also depended on Byrd's drift indicator, which informed them how to adjust for the blowing wind.

They flew at 2,000 feet, and though they could see fifty miles away, they spied no land. There were only ice packs below and occasionally patches of water. Byrd made out areas down below which men had laboriously crossed in their heroic efforts to reach the Pole on foot. The Arctic was no continent, only a sea of ice, and somewhere within it where all the longitudinal lines met at one point lay the North Pole.

They were only an hour from the Pole, according to Byrd's calculations, when a fearful decision had to be made. Glancing through the cabin window, Byrd discovered a flow of leaking oil from one motor. "That motor will stop," Bennett told him. He proposed that they attempt a landing and repair the motor.

"Let's wait a while," said Byrd. "We won't be any worse off if we land nearer the Pole than we will be if we land here." Bennett agreed uneasily, with one eye on the oil-pressure indicator.

They kept flying north, expecting any moment that the motor would stop. Suddenly at 9:02 A.M. on that day of May 9, Byrd's calculations showed they were on top of the world at the Pole. They circled in a wide sweep to make certain they had covered the Pole. No great emotion overcame them. Instead, said Byrd, he felt "impersonal, disembodied."

After a while they started back. Flying over the Pole had taken their minds off the leaking motor. Now their thoughts were once more back to their immediate problem. But a miracle occurred. Suddenly the leaking stopped. A rivet had come loose from its hole and when the oil level dropped below the hole the leaking stopped.

When they were over Kings Bay again, the *Chantier* let out a loud whistle. Once on the ground, their men swooped them up on their shoulders and laughed with happiness.

Captain Amundsen proved a good sport. He congratulated Byrd and asked, "Well, Byrd, what shall it be now?"

"The South Pole," Byrd replied.

"A big job," said Amundsen, "but it can be done."

Byrd had no idea that his flight across the North Pole would make his name a household word. Back in the United States every newspaper headlined his feat. In large letters, the headline of *The New York Times* announced:

BYRD FLIES TO NORTH POLE AND BACK;
ROUND TRIP FROM KINGS BAY IN 15 HRS. 51 MIN;
CIRCLES TOP OF WORLD SEVERAL TIMES

A hero's welcome was accorded him and Bennett on their return to the United States. New York gave them its biggest parade in history. Congress awarded both the Congressional Medal of Honor. President Coolidge said of Byrd: "We cannot but admire the superb courage of the man willing to set forth on such a great adventure in the unexplored realms of the air. . . . His deed will be but the beginning of scientific exploration considered difficult of achievement before he proved the possibilities of the airplane."

Byrd's older brother Harry, who was now Governor of Virginia, welcomed him back to his native state. But it was his return to Winchester on July 14 that gave Byrd his greatest thrill. He was still "Little Dick" to the townspeople, and his daring accomplishment, said many, was something that could have been foretold in his youth.

Chapter 7

SPANNING THE ATLANTIC

ALTHOUGH Byrd had mentioned to Amundsen that he planned to fly over the South Pole, there was a more immediate project he wanted to complete first. This was a flight across the Atlantic to Europe.

The NC-4 had made such a flight in four steps in 1919. An airship, the R-34, a British dirigible, had also gone that year from England to New York and back. What

Byrd had in mind was a nonstop flight by airplane from New York to Europe.

After the tumult following their flight across the North Pole had subsided somewhat, Byrd and Bennett began seriously to plan their flight across the Atlantic. By a special act of Congress, Byrd was named a commander on the Navy's retired list and Bennett was advanced to warrant machinist. Though this title sounded insignificant so far as Bennett was concerned, the aviation industry nevertheless recognized him as the best pilot in the country.

When Byrd and Bennett discussed their projected flight with aeronautical experts, they were advised to fly a single-engine plane. Such a plane would have greater cruising range and would be cheaper and simpler to operate than a multi-engine plane. "But I want a three-motor plane," said Byrd. "Going by a single-engine plane would be a stunt because it would have no long-range value. The success of a multi-engine plane would open the door of the future to commercial transatlantic flights."

Rodman Wanamaker, who was in the department store business and a leading enthusiast for flying, agreed to provide Byrd with a plane such as he had in mind. However, Wanamaker laid down the condition that Byrd and Bennett should attempt to reach Paris. He hoped in this way to create good will between the United States and France. The plane must also be named the *America*.

Late in 1926 construction of the *America* began. It was a large plane with a wingspread of 71 feet. Byrd planned to take three or four others besides himself and Bennett to prove that nonoperating passengers could make a comfortable trip across the ocean. The plane was also made larger in order to carry special equipment to ensure safety.

Byrd spent months planning every possible detail that would make the flight a success. For example, he built a special 1,200-gallon gas tank. On it he put the first dump valve used in planes, a device to empty the fuel in seconds if the plane were heading for a crash. The special tank would also float if they were forced down at sea. Byrd also carried a waterproof radio set and a powerful automatic sending device that would flash a radio signal every six seconds across the Atlantic. There were in addition special rubber boats that could be inflated easily, as well as emergency food, clothing, and signal devices. At Byrd's urging, the U. S. Weather Bureau began making regular weather maps of the North Atlantic.

By the beginning of 1927 strong excitement had developed throughout the United States at the prospect of a nonstop flight across the Atlantic. The Orteig Prize of $25,000 was offered to the first plane to reach Paris. Dozens of pilots were working feverishly to win this award, and more than thirty lives were to be lost that year on that account. Byrd specifically made it clear he was not in the race; that what he wanted to do was to make a pioneer flight in a commercial-type airplane.

On April 20, the *America* was ready for air-testing. Byrd insisted on flying aloft during the test, even though many friends argued that it was a needless risk.

Anton Fokker, the great Dutch plane designer who produced the *America,* was at the controls, while Byrd, Bennett, and George Noville, a pilot and radio operator, went along as observers. The take-off was smooth, but once the plane was in the air Byrd noticed that Bennett was licking his lips. He always did this when something was amiss.

When the plane came down for the landing, the front end dipped low while the tail shot up. Fokker immediately took the plane upward again, though by now Byrd knew why Bennett had licked his lips. The plane was nose-heavy.

With little fuel remaining, Fokker had no alternative other than to land. As the plane came in at sixty miles an hour, Byrd braced himself behind Fokker's seat and said a prayer. Just as the wheels touched the runway, Fokker leaped through the plane's only exit. Then came a horrible crash as the plane turned turtle and slammed down upside down. Byrd suffered harsh blows to his head and back and his left arm bones snapped, when Noville piled into him. Wildly, Noville punched a hole in the side of the fuselage with a fist and fell out of the plane, badly injured internally.

Despite his wounds, Byrd hurried to Bennett. Floyd was hanging with his head down, his eyes filled with oil and one leg broken. Byrd's first thought was that this was Bennett's finish. "Guess I'm done for," Bennett said quietly between gasps. "I'm all broken up. I can't see and I have no feeling in my left arm."

"You'll be all right, old man," Byrd assured him weakly.

Neither Bennett nor Noville was expected to live, said the doctor to Byrd as they were being rushed to the hospital. Along the way Byrd set his own broken arm. Both Bennett and Noville recovered, though Bennett's injuries took so long to heal that he dropped all hope of taking part in a transatlantic flight.

It took a month to repair the damage to the *America*. By this time several fliers were preparing to hop across the Atlantic. Graciously, Byrd offered advice to one young flier named Charles Lindbergh and made his own excellent air field available to Lindbergh. On May 20, when Lindbergh prepared to take off in early morning from Byrd's Roosevelt Field on Long Island, Byrd was on hand to wish him good luck.

It was on June 29, more than a month after Lindbergh's successful crossing, that Byrd was ready for his own flight. Instead of Floyd Bennett, Bert Acosta would serve as pilot. Bernt Balchen, a young Norwegian, was assistant pilot and George Noville radio operator. Byrd reached Roosevelt Field at three A.M. in a light rain, yet an enormous crowd was on hand to watch the take-off. Last-hour preparations had kept Byrd awake for twenty-three hours, yet the excitement of the coming trip held him alert. "The worst thing that can happen to us," Byrd told his old friend Admiral Moffett of the Navy, "is to reach Paris in darkness, and fog and storm."

Little did he realize that what he said in jest would come true. His trip across the Atlantic was to prove his most hair-raising experience. First the stout rope that held the plane in place while the motors warmed up broke. This meant that the plane roared toward its take-off ahead of plans. As the plane neared the end of the runway without rising, Acosta started the signal for Noville to press the dump valve and empty the gas tank. But before this could be accomplished, the plane suddenly lurched and its wheels left the runway. They were off to Europe!

Once in the air, the *America* ran headlong into heavy rain and fog. The plane grew steadily colder and Byrd feared that ice would form on the wings and propeller. To

forestall this situation the plane had to fly at a higher altitude. Yet if this were done steadily, it would result in
a higher rate of gas consumption, and they would run out
of fuel before reaching France. One time when Byrd
worried about this possibility, he glanced over to find
Balchen sleeping with his foot almost against the handle
of the dump valve.

The 2,000-mile flight was made with only rare glimpses
of the ocean below them. Again, as on the North Pole
flight, a leak occurred, this time in the gas tank. But Byrd
had brought along some putty and he quickly applied it.
They flew by radio bearings and from signals from passing
ocean steamers below. Later on, signals came to them from
radio sending stations all over Europe.

Flying was so difficult in the inky weather that though
Byrd, Acosta, and Balchen took turns flying, the strain on
all of them was great. The second night they were over the
Atlantic a strange event took place. It came at a time when
they were nearing the French coast. Acosta was piloting
and he began muttering that there was a fifth man in the
plane. In his drowsiness, he had turned the plane about
and instead of heading for Paris, he was flying back toward
New York. The plane was quickly turned back on course
by Balchen and Byrd.

When a turning beam of light flashed below them, Byrd
was convinced they were reaching Paris. However, a
closer look the next time the light revolved showed they
were over a lighthouse on the coast of France. But Paris
was not far inland and joyously they sped toward their
final destination.

However, this was not to be because they found Paris

enveloped in a punishing storm. "We can't take a chance and land at Le Bourget Field," Byrd told his companions. "In this soup, we'll probably crash into people on the ground." The alternative was dismal, but there was no other choice.

Back to the coastal lighthouse they flew with Balchen piloting. Byrd had hoped they could land on the beach. But the heavy rain and fog prevented this. They would have to crash-land in the water.

When the plane hit the water, the wheels broke off and the fuselage began filling with water. Noville broke a window and swam out into the darkness. Byrd received a harsh blow over his heart and for a long time afterward it did not beat regularly. Nevertheless, Byrd swam forward into the cockpit and helped Balchen pull himself free. Acosta was already outside and swimming for his life, even though he had suffered a broken collarbone.

Noville had torn into the emergency cabin and extricated a rubber boat. Then after it was inflated, the four rowed to shore. But even here their troubles were not over. Soaking wet, they had to walk a mile to the village of Ver-sur-Mer. Once in the village, they found all gates outside the houses locked. A boy on a bicycle took one look at them, thought they were hoodlums and pedaled for his life. In the end, they were taken in by the lighthouse keeper and his wife.

Later Byrd returned to the *America* to save his records of the flight and a bag of mail. It was important for him to save the mail because he had been entrusted with the first transatlantic mail in air history.

The welcome he and his men received in Paris rivaled

the New York celebration when he and Floyd Bennett returned from their flight over the North Pole. Crowds everywhere cheered wildly, and the four men were made citizens of several cities.

Despite the mishap at the end of his flight, Byrd knew that he had blazoned a path for transoceanic commercial air flights. It would be only a matter of time before there would be steady traffic across the Atlantic.

Chapter 8

SOUTH TO THE ANTARCTIC

Now that Commander Byrd had realized his ambition to make a nonstop flight across the Atlantic Ocean, his thoughts turned to the Antarctic Continent. Here lay man's last great physical frontier on the face of the globe and Byrd meant to conquer it in the name of his country.

This would be no small feat, he knew, considering that remote Antarctica had the most hostile climate in the world. In some places there, winds were reported to blow at 200 miles an hour. Temperatures could easily drop below −100°F. The antarctic winter was a sunless world, forbidding and dark and filled with dangerous crevasses. In the summer the sun circled the sky continuously. Not a tree grew on the entire continent, though on its outer edges penguins, seals, whales, and birds abounded. Unlike the arctic region where Eskimos lived, the Antarctic had not a single living person.

According to the deep research Byrd made of the Antarctic, man's efforts there had been meager. During the Middle Ages, map makers insisted that there must be a southern continent. They called it Terra Australis Incognita, and said that millions of people lived there who enjoyed great wealth and an excellent climate.

With this incentive, daring explorers began pushing out from Europe in search of this southern continent. Vasco da Gama and Sir Francis Drake were two who sailed off with bright hopes. But below America and Africa they saw only water that seemed to go on forever. In time the hunt went on from Australia and New Zealand. In 1773, the renowned explorer Captain James Cook sailed south of the Antarctic Circle, though he did not spy the continent. He quit when he feared being trapped by icebergs and the dangerous pack ice. It was this voyage that proved conclusively that a warm southern continent was only a myth, even if there was actually a continent below the Sixtieth Parallel.

It was on November 17, 1820, that a twenty-year-old American seal captain named Nathaniel Palmer claimed he saw the rim of an ice continent. He said he did not go ashore because the ice was too treacherous, though from his ship he traveled along the north coast of West Antarctica. At that time the American Government had no interest in claiming Palmer's discovered continent.

During the 1830's, the American, British and French governments sent expeditions to the antarctic region to locate the South Magnetic Pole. Ship navigators found that their compasses moved erratically because of the pull from that Pole, and its location would make possible more accurate maps. Lt. Charles Wilkes, who led the American expedition, was later court-martialed on the ground that he had made false geographic claims. In truth, he hadn't, though he was as far off as fifty miles in some calculations of what he saw from his ship.

There is some dispute as to who first set foot on Antarctica. It is known, however, that a Norwegian expedition stepped on shore in 1894. The following year a daring British-Norwegian party spent a winter in a little wood shack on the rim of the continent.

After this, men were determined to reach the South Pole where all the lines of longitude meet. All such attempts were made from the side of Antarctica closest to New Zealand, a distance of about 800 wild miles over mountains, glaciers and crevasses. British Captain Robert F. Scott attempted this first in 1901–1904 but failed. Then came Ernest Shackleton, another Britisher, who came within 97 miles of the Pole in January, 1909, before he had to turn back.

The following year two expeditions competed in the contest to reach the magic spot. One, led by Roald Amundsen of Norway, made a quick dash by dog team, sleds and skis. Amundsen planted a flag at the South Pole on December 14, 1911, and scurried back as swiftly as he could travel.

Captain Scott, who had come again, forged ahead with ponies. Unfortunately, ponies could not withstand the climate and the Scott party of five were forced to hand-haul their heavy sledges. When they reached the Pole on January 17, 1912, their spirit gave way when they discovered Amundsen's black flag. "The Pole . . . Great God!" Scott wrote in his diary. "This is an awful place and terrible enough for us to have laboured to it without the reward of priority. . . . Now for the run home and a desperate struggle. I wonder if we can do it."

The Scott party could not do it. Only eleven miles from a food depot and less than one hundred and fifty miles from their warm home base, they perished. "Had we lived," wrote Scott before dying, "I should have a tale to tell of the hardiness, endurance and courage of my companions."

It was a place such as this that Commander Byrd was intent on subduing in the name of his country.

After he returned from France, he set out in earnest to prepare for his expedition south. Floyd Bennett was well on the road to recovery now and Byrd named him second in command of the projected expedition. "There is no man in the world I would rather go into the Antarctic with than you," he told Bennett. Bennett accepted the offer with satisfaction.

When Lt. Wilkes sailed for the Antarctic in the 1830's, his expedition had been sponsored by the American Government. However, Byrd was unable to awaken governmental interest in his expedition. As a result, he had to turn again to friends to help defray his expenses. A trip such as the one he had in mind would cost $750,000, or perhaps more.

At the end of 1927, he established an office in New York as headquarters for himself and Bennett. Here he prepared a detailed list of the equipment he would require. First he needed two ships to carry his crew and gear south. Short of money, he bought two old sea travelers, though he found after rerigging and reoutfitting that their expense came to the enormous sum of $290,000. One was an old sailing ship built originally in 1882, which he renamed the *City of New York*. The other was a slow-moving tramp steamer, which after repainting he christened the *Eleanor Bolling*, after his mother.

He also bought four airplanes, all ski-equipped monoplanes, though one had to be left behind. His expedition would have a twofold purpose: to fly over the South Pole and to conduct scientific investigations. For the flight across the Pole, he purchased the most modern plane then in existence, a large all-metal three-engined plane with the ability to fly 122 miles an hour and carry a load of 15,000 pounds. He had also to buy 665 tons of assorted cargo and 100 dogs. In addition, he would take along about forty men who would winter on the Antarctic and a like number to man his two ships. With thousands of volunteers to select from, he had his pick of brawny scientists, almost all of whom agreed to come along at the pay of one dollar a year.

Raising money was a heartache. Some came from the pennies sent him by school children; other money came from anonymous sources. But chief support came from Edsel Ford and John D. Rockefeller, Jr. Even so, by mid-1928 he was $300,000 in debt. When he finally left the United States on his expedition, it was with the heavy concern that he still owed suppliers $100,000.

But money was not his only disheartening concern. In the spring of 1928, two German fliers crashed on Greenly Island in the Gulf of St. Lawrence. Floyd Bennett decided to take time off from expedition details and flew to their rescue. He came out with a bad cold that required hospitalization in Quebec. Then came the stunning news to Byrd on April twenty-fifth that Bennett had died of pneumonia.

Byrd was disconsolate and for a while his Antarctic expedition lost its meaning. But gradually he returned to his planning and fund raising. In memory of his best friend he named his South Pole plane the *Floyd Bennett*. Said Byrd: "His death deprived me of a judgment, loyalty and determination in which I always had implicit faith."

On August 25, 1928, the *City of New York* left the United States for New Zealand by way of the Panama Canal. A month later the *Eleanor Bolling* made her departure. Byrd traveled across the United States and went to New Zealand aboard the *C. A. Larson,* a whaling factory ship, steaming from California. At Dunedin in New Zealand, he planned a rendezvous with his two ships for the 2,500-mile journey to Antarctica.

Speed was essential to Byrd because he had to have his camp in operation long before the winter night's four months of darkness fell the following April. In the Antarctic it was wise to arrive in November to prepare one's camp. Then when the winter night began and no outside work was possible, the men would be safely indoors. During the winter night, the explorers would make final preparations for whatever activities they planned when the sun reappeared.

It was therefore with agony that Byrd watched the slow progress of the *City of New York*. The sailing ship required thirty days to reach the Panama Canal, a trip that was done ordinarily in a week or so. At Panama a crisis developed. Byrd had not anticipated the need of money to pay for toll charges and coal. When the canal captain demanded cash, the voyage appeared doomed. Fortunately, one of the sailors aboard the *City* was heir to a large fortune. Begrimed from his duties, he casually handed over the necessary cash and the ship was permitted to go on. The *City of New York* finally reached New Zealand after one hundred days at sea.

It was on December 2 that Byrd walked up the gangway of the *City of New York*. His two ships were ready for the 2,500-mile voyage to the Antarctic. Both ships were so low in the water because of their heavy cargoes that New Zealanders warned Byrd he would never reach his destination. But Byrd was not to be halted at this point. He was to learn before his trip ended why the various latitude zones had their odd names. From forty to fifty degrees south latitude, that area was known as the "Roaring Forties." Then came the "Furious Fifties," and after this the "Screaming Sixties." The heavy seas and fierce winds almost ripped his ships apart.

From New Zealand southward, the weather grew increasingly worse. On the ninth of December, Byrd saw his first iceberg. An occasional iceberg he saw later on was as large as the state of Connecticut. From his research Byrd knew he was well on the way to the ice pack. This is a belt of drifting ice, which in some seasons is 600 miles wide.

Now as the ships poked their noses gingerly through the first pieces of drifting ice and around icebergs, Byrd grew concerned. He had made arrangements with the captain of the whaler *Larson* to tow the *City* through the ice pack. But with that ship approaching the South Magnetic Pole, the *City*'s compasses shivered erratically. It was only by taking radio bearings on the wireless waves sent out by the *Larson* that the two ships finally met.

Before the *Larson* slung her 3½-inch single wire towing cable over the *City*'s bow on December 15, an 80-foot-long blue whale came crashing through the ice and water. But an expert harpoon gunner soon dispatched the 90-ton monster with well-placed hits. The whale was then hauled aboard the *Larson* and cut up for its crude oil and food.

It took a week for the *Larson* to hack a narrow path for the *City* through the ice pack. With the ice several feet thick, this was a jarring experience for Byrd and his men aboard the *City*. Besides the danger of the ice ramming into the stern of the *Larson,* there was the harrowing problem of heavy ice broken off by the *Larson* re-forming behind her and smashing the little *City*.

At last, however, on the twenty-first, the ice pack lay behind and the *City* emerged into the quiet blue Ross Sea. Pushing on southward through this placid sea, Byrd came at last to one of the most impressive sights he had ever witnessed. Here was the Ross Ice Barrier, a sheer 100-foot-high ice cliff that formed the edge of the continent.

Since there was no safe way to scale this wall and land supplies, Byrd moved eastward alongside it for 400 miles. Here he came at last to the Bay of Whales, a twenty-mile break in the barrier wall. Named appropriately after the many whales who commanded the vicinity, the Bay of Whales afforded a gradual ascent to the barrier top. Amundsen had used the bay as his home base for his successful dash to the Pole.

With prayerful thanks for his safe arrival, Byrd climbed down the Jacob's-ladder slung over the bow of the ship and set off in search of a campsite. Byrd went off by dog team and skis up the gentle incline from the bay to the barrier top, and returned the following day. "I found an excellent campsite on level ice eight miles from here," he told his crew.

He christened his camp Little America, though it resembled no place in the United States. Now began the task of unloading his supplies and constructing his village. Gear was lowered to the bay ice and the hundred Eskimo dogs covered more than 12,000 miles in a relentless shuttle operation from the bay to Little America. Most difficult was the task of hauling the planes, a backbreaking job even without the misery of blinding snowstorms.

Throughout the unloading, the watchful eyes of penguins and seals took in the show. There were the 80-pound emperor penguins, highly dignified in appearance, as if they were prepared to attend formal balls. There were also the comical little Adélie penguins who slid over the ice on their stomachs. The 8-foot seals were dull creatures who basked in bored fashion under the 24-hour sun.

But the killer whales were different. Forty or fifty of

them were generally in sight, and their ugly faces and small beady eyes remained constantly on the lookout for trouble. On one occasion, Byrd and a few of his men were in a small boat when several 25-foot killer whales came after them. Just in time the men leaped onto a piece of ice. Byrd pulled out a revolver as a last-ditch measure should the whales follow. But for some unexplained reason the whales went off in another direction. Afterward Byrd laughed. "These bullets would not even have dented their hides."

Despite the lurking dangers during the unloading, only once was there serious trouble. This occurred when the *Bolling* rested close to the continent's edge and the barrier wall collapsed suddenly, and showered her with hundreds of tons of ice. The steamer fell over on her side, but like a game fighter, she slowly righted herself.

Byrd, who had watched this seeming catastrophe from the deck of the *City,* sighed with relief when the *Bolling* returned upright. But then a shout went out. "Man overboard!' Without hesitating, Byrd rushed to the rail and dived overboard despite his knowledge that no one could survive longer than six minutes in Antarctica's frigid waters. Both Byrd and the sailor were finally rescued by crewmen in small boats. Byrd returned shivering violently to the *City.* Said an eyewitness: "Part of this episode was caught by the alert movie-men, but their request for several re-takes to complete the scenario was repulsed by the commander."

The village of Little America consisted of three chief buildings—the Mess Hall, Administration Building and the Norwegian House. There were also about a dozen other small buildings, such as bunkhouses, machine shops, and a radio shack, as well as hangars for the planes. These were mainly portable buildings that came in sections for joining, because the construction of regular buildings would be too difficult in the antarctic climate. Byrd's plan of construction was to dig holes four feet deep in the ice and then bolt the building sections together on that anchor. He knew that snowdrifts would soon submerge his camp and, free from winds blowing over the surface, his buildings would be warmer than if they were above the ice. Even so, ice came up through floor cracks, mattresses froze and indoor morning temperatures read a shivering $-30°F$.

The camp was in smooth operation long before the four-month winter night fell on April 22. Within a month after his arrival at Little America, Byrd flew on his first exploratory flight in the Antarctic. Along his route into the unknown, he flew over a mountain range, a discovery he named the Rockefeller Mountains. Several of the scientists in camp meanwhile broke out their scientific gear and made preliminary studies of the weather, the snow, and the animals in the bay.

However, the winter night was soon upon them and the men were forced to remain in camp. Fortunately, Byrd was an excellent leader and organizer and cramped living did not bring on trouble. He provided his crew with a superb library, a gymnasium and a variety of tasks to keep them busy. One of the biggest jobs was making water, for though the Antarctic is covered with ice, it is actually a desert. A man caught outdoors would soon die of thirst because the cold weather would not permit him to melt the snow. This had to be done in a heated snow melter, a laborious job indeed. Another task that consumed a great deal of time during the winter night was the beehive of preparation for the coming springtime scientific investigations and Byrd's proposed flight over the South Pole almost eight hundred miles away.

Byrd's ability as a leader showed up well during the four months of darkness. He made suggestions and did not give orders. He also treated all the men alike, no matter how distinguished some of them had been back in the United States. So far as he was concerned there was no such thing as rank. A man's worth depended on how he acted at Little America.

Byrd also did not believe that a leader should punish a man for behaving poorly. Instead, he believed that the group would soon straighten out a man who acted in an obnoxious fashion. However, if the group went too far, it was then time for the leader to step in and bring everyone back to normal. In addition, Byrd believed that a leader had to be aloof from the group and show no favoritism. The men had to feel that their leader was superior to them, and in Byrd's case this was not too difficult.

If there was a problem during that winter night, it arose over food. The barreled beef he had brought along turned rancid. But the meat problem was solved by the abundance of penguins and seals. However, vegetables were a more serious matter. Byrd had purchased large quantities of dehydrated vegetables that were inedible. He learned later that his vegetables were dehydrated during World War I, more than ten years before.

Nevertheless, the men did not waste away and when spring came late in August, they were ready for their various enterprises. The biggest of these was Byrd's proposed flight to the Pole. The temperature having risen from the winter's low of −72.2° to a warm −40°, the men worked joyously digging out the tri-motored *Floyd Bennett*. Then came several trial flights to arouse the cold motors, plus more careful planning of routes and supplies.

About halfway between Little America and the South Pole lies a vast mountain range called the Queen Maud Range. Some of its peaks rise as high as 15,000 feet. Beyond the Queen Maud Range lies a high plateau in which sits the Geographic South Pole, a point resting on almost a two-mile thickness of snow. A forced landing almost anywhere along this route could mean death unless full precautions were taken.

With this in mind, Byrd made several exploration flights toward the Queen Maud Range to study the terrain. On a flight on November 18, he landed at the foot of the range at Liv Glacier, a 45-mile pass through the Queen Mauds. Here he built a depot and deposited within it food, oil, fuel, and a stove. If he reached the Pole from Little America, he planned to stop at Liv Glacier on his return to take on the fuel. For his plane could not carry enough fuel for a nonstop round-trip flight, in view of the extremely high elevation. As an added precaution, a geological party on its way to the Queen Maud Range to explore also laid down a string of depots along its route. This ground party was also to report from the range when the weather was sufficiently clear for a flight over the mountains.

The signal came on Thanksgiving Day and at three P.M. on November 28, the *Floyd Bennett* wobbled off the rough ice runway at Little America. There were three others in the plane besides Byrd, who served as navigator. Bernt Balchen, who had flown with him across the Atlantic, served as pilot; Harold June as co-pilot and radio operator; and Ashley McKinley as aerial photographer.

As they flew southward over crevasses and the barren ice, Byrd's concern was whether the heavily laden plane would have the power to fly over the mountains. Onward they flew at 90 miles an hour and at 8:15 they passed over the geological party below them. A friendly wave to the men below and then it was all concentration on crossing the "hump" that lay ahead.

By 9:15 they reached Liv Glacier and began the climb over this mountain pass. Liv was a treacherous chasm filled with rough ice and wide crevasses. The air was rough, too, and the wind beat against the plane with fury. When they had passed the ten-mile point inside narrowing Liv, it became apparent that the plane would have to fly higher or crash into the glacier. But the plane was already straining at its ceiling.

Balchen suddenly yelled out with desperation, "Overboard—overboard—200 pounds!"

Only if the plane were made lighter could it gain elevation. Byrd had to act swiftly. But what would it be—gasoline or food? If he threw out gasoline, they could not make it to the Pole and back to their cache. But if they threw out food, their lives would be endangered if they were forced down.

Byrd looked at his three companions and weighed his decision. "Harold, a bag of food overboard!" he called out to June.

The plane rose noticeably. "More!" shouted Balchen, as he saw that the plane was still flying below the top of the pass.

Another bag of food followed. The plane jumped almost 400 feet immediately. All the food was gone now, but the plane made it over the hump.

They were now on the polar plateau, some three hundred miles from the Pole. The rest of the flight was without incident. At 1:14 A.M. on November 29, 1929, the plane hovered over the same bleak spot where Amundsen and Scott had trekked. Over the Pole, Byrd opened a trap door and dropped an American flag weighted by a stone from Floyd Bennett's grave. "The flag had been advanced 1,500 miles farther south than it had ever been," wrote Byrd. As for the Pole area itself, Byrd called it "only a white desolation and solitude."

On his return to Little America, Byrd went off on several other exploratory flights where no man had ever been before. One vast area he named Marie Byrd Land after his wife. Another mountain range whose peaks reached to 10,000 feet he called the Edsel Ford Range. Byrd's aerial cameras permitted him to map more of the Antarctic than had all the expeditions preceding his. Of his party's scientific findings, most important was the discovery of coal on the higher mountains of the Queen Maud Range. This gave evidence that at an earlier age the Antarctic was not covered with ice, but was instead warm enough to hold trees and vegetation.

In February of 1930, Byrd departed from the Antarctic with the hope that his efforts there had awakened in the American people an interest in that continent. He was therefore surprised to find on his return to the United States that he had become a symbol for the Antarctic. Everywhere he was treated as a conquering hero, even though he said he had merely scratched the surface of antarctic exploration.

Said President Herbert Hoover to him: "I know that I speak for the American people when I express their universal pleasure at your successful flight over the South Pole. We are proud of your courage and your leadership. We are glad of proof that the spirit of great adventure lives."

Chapter 9

A DEEPER LOOK AT ANTARCTICA

BYRD's soul did crave adventure. But it was more than this that led him to concentrate his efforts on the Antarctic. Only the tiniest portion of the Antarctic's 5,000,000 square miles had ever been glimpsed by man. Byrd meant to fit the missing pieces into the map. He was also determined to explore the possible resources of the ice continent. What other ores were there besides coal? How could man make use of its strategic nearness to the bottoms of

South America, Africa, and Australia? Did the Antarctic's weather affect the climate of other areas on the globe?

These and a host of other questions were on his mind. For instance, how could he establish a claim for his country for the areas he discovered in the Antarctic? Other nations claimed parts of the Antarctic their explorers had never sighted. Yet the American Government seemed reluctant to push its frontiers out farther than they were at the moment.

All these matters Byrd considered carefully and at length. What he faced was a lifetime devoted to the Antarctic if he were to achieve his goals. However, he had no alternatives. Besides, he liked what he called the "pull of discovery." This made his task easier, for as he admitted, "No one who has ever seen new lands rising above the prow of a ship, or above a running dog team, or through the shine of a propeller, can easily deny the pull."

Almost as soon as Byrd set foot on American soil after his first Antarctic expedition, he began preparing plans for his return. There were his large debts to repay and a nationwide lecturing schedule to fulfill. But he was paid as much as $1,500 for a talk, and within a year he paid off the last of his creditors. Byrd now lived with his wife, his son, and three daughters in a five-story, ivy-covered brick house on Brimmer Street in Boston's Back Bay. This house was soon a beehive of activity as he prepared for his second assault on the Antarctic.

While Byrd had been away on his first expedition, Congress had elevated him in rank to a rear admiral on the retired list. This plus his widespread fame should have made his money-raising task fairly simple. However, this was not the case. The country was then deeply mired in an economic depression. Millions of workers could not find jobs; businesses were failing by the thousands each month; and banks could not pay depositors.

Byrd's original hope for a million-dollar expedition could not be realized under these circumstances. Putting his own money into his enterprise, plus the donations he managed to raise, he had a total of $150,000. Nevertheless, he was able to wheedle valuable supplies directly from manufacturers at no cost. Colleges and government agencies lent him scientific equipment worth $100,000. Among the 30,000 business firms Byrd wrote to for aid, many agreed to supply him with their wares if he would let them advertise that fact. With no alternative, Byrd agreed to this demand. As a result, he got his necessary oil, windproof cloth, coal, stoves, motors, shoes, and meat. For other vital funds, he also sold the radio rights for regular broadcasts from the Antarctic to the United States to the Columbia Broadcasting System.

This was a task Admiral Byrd disliked intensely and it had its embarrassing moments. For instance, he sent almost one hundred and fifty letters to firms that made overalls, with hope of getting a free supply. Not a single company offered as much as one pair. It was only after a year of corresponding with lumber yards that he wore down the resistance of one yard owner and won a donation of vital hickory for his sledges.

His worst experience occurred with the procurement of an icebreaker. He needed two ships—a steamer and an icebreaker. The steamer he rented from the United States Shipping Board for one dollar a year, and named her the

Jacob Ruppert, after one of his contributors who owned a brewery and the New York Yankees baseball team. With hundreds of World War I freight boats sitting idly in ports, the Shipping Board was happy to have one of its ships in use.

As for his icebreaker to slice through the ice pack, Byrd had his eye on a sturdy vessel owned by the city of Oakland in California. Built in 1884, this ship had belonged to the Coast Guard and had taken part in the Yukon gold rush in 1898. Oakland authorities agreed to let Byrd have the ship for a few dollars, but the sale could be completed legally only at public auction. Unfortunately, a junkman appeared at the auction and made it known that he would like to buy the ship and tear her apart for scrap. After Byrd worriedly made his token bid, the junkman shouted, "I bid one thousand dollars." Stern talk followed which resulted in the junkman's agreement finally not to bid higher. Nevertheless, his bid could not be retracted and Byrd was forced to pay $1,050 from his meager purse.

If he had such trying moments, he also had his joys. Again he was blessed with an excess of eager top scientists and sailors who were willing to go along at a salary of one dollar a year. Many who accompanied him on his first expedition stoutly insisted during that stay that one expedition was enough. Now he found them camped at his doorway and pleading for the chance to go again. Some who could not go insisted nevertheless on helping him prepare his departure. Dr. Dana Coman, medical officer on his first expedition, dragged heavy loads as a stevedore on the *Ruppert* before she left the country.

It was during the fall of 1933 that all the bits and pieces

were in place and the Second Byrd Antarctic Expedition
sailed southward. But hardly had the *Bear,* as Byrd christened the Oakland icebreaker, slipped her mooring when
the expedition almost came to a close. Off Southport,
North Carolina, a wild hurricane buffeted the *Bear* and
a raging sea rushed over her bow and flooded her holds
and engine room. But she managed to stay upright and
lasted out the storm.

Byrd sailed aboard the *Ruppert,* which was to rendezvous with the *Bear* in the Bay of Whales three months
later. It was Byrd's intention to use the trip to the Antarctic as a major bit of air exploration. Once through the
Panama Canal, the *Ruppert* was to travel down the coast
of South America to Peter I Island, a dot of land inside
the Antarctic Circle. From the island, Byrd planned a nonstop flight in a giant Condor biplane all the way westward
to Little America. Thus he hoped to map a large stretch
of unknown territory.

However, as the *Ruppert* steamed down the Pacific side
of South America, the U. S. Army sent him word that the
Condor's propellers were structurally weak. Without hesi-
tation, Byrd altered course immediately for Wellington,
New Zealand. From a daredevil youth, he had matured
into a cautious explorer. Taking needless chances was the
mark of stupidity and not bravery.

It was on December eleventh that the *Ruppert* left New
Zealand for Antarctica. Despite last-minute tasks that went
clear around the clock during the six days' stay in New
Zealand, Byrd felt relaxed. This was not like his first
venture. What he faced in the period ahead he believed he

could foretell generally. He was to find that the Antarctic was a land of continual surprises.

In the passage south toward Antarctica, the pack ice belt proved surprisingly narrow this time. However, the number of icebergs almost proved overwhelming. In a single day the crew spied more than 8,000. Byrd dubbed the area where the icebergs were most numerous "The Devil's Graveyard." Throughout frenzied nights came loud warning calls from lookouts in the crow's-nest high above deck: "Berg off the starboard bow!" or "Berg close to port!" And then the ship would groan and turn to avoid fatal collision. Sometimes the icebergs turned out to be mirages.

Eventually, the *Ruppert* moved into the Ross Sea again and steamed eastward along the high ice-barrier edge of the continent. At 9:15 A.M. on January 17, the break in the barrier wall known as the Bay of Whales hove into view. "We are home again," Byrd told his crew as he pointed to the familiar sight.

Little America was still recognizable and the approach seemed easier. For the ship was able to maneuver in the bay to within three miles of the base, unlike the eight miles on the first expedition. Joyous at this change, Byrd set off to see whether his old base could be used again.

One sharp glance told him he would have to build a new base. Only a few antenna poles, radio towers, smokestacks and ventilators were in sight. Five years had completely buried the buildings of the former village. Probing the snow, four feet below the surface Byrd reached the top of his old Administration Building. Inside he found a thick ice crystal coating everywhere. Beams had cracked and the roof sagged. But on the mess-hall table was a big roast put there four years before. The cold had preserved it so that it had not spoiled during that long period. Other usable food lay frozen in pans on the stove.

However, the glee in uncovering old memories soon faded. For real trouble was at hand. The separated barrier walls that produced the opening known as the Bay of Whales were slowly closing. The result was that pressure ice formed by this process ground the bay into an impassable area. There was no way to cut a trail through the pressure ice to Little America. Indeed, the place had become wild with solid waves of ice, some peaks of which rose thirty to fifty feet.

There was only one answer to the problem of unloading supplies. Instead of a three-mile haul to camp, there would be a twenty-mile trip skirting the pressure ice in the bay. "Misery Trail," the men called their long haul. Time was running out now because little was left of the antarctic summer and there was so much work to do. In the Antarctic, Byrd had learned, "time was always the master and you were its creature." For almost three weeks, the men and dogs worked at least eighteen hours a day through fog and blizzard to bring supplies from ship to camp. Some grew so weary that they could not talk or eat properly. Others suffered frostbites and snow blindness. Just when the men felt they could no longer continue, the *Bear* appeared in the Bay of Whales and her men pitched in to help.

Even when the supplies were unloaded at Little America, the job was not finished. Byrd realized that his first camp was not safe and ordered the construction of Little America II on top of Little America I. The second camp amounted to eight buildings to house the 56-man expedition and contained connecting passageways between the old and new camp.

Then when the new camp was completed, Byrd took a stroll and discovered that the ice had cracked in the area surrounding the camp. If these cracks deepened, the entire camp would float out to sea! For safety, Byrd aroused his weary crew in a further effort to store an emergency supply of gear about a mile farther inland. But the growing cold sealed the cracks and made this effort unnecessary.

After all this bad luck, the men agreed there should be clear sailing ahead. But the ill fortune had yet to run its full course. One of the expedition's four planes was involved in a crash. A building caught fire and valuable equipment was barely saved. "Good Lord! What now?" was Byrd's comment. The question was answered in the form of another emergency. One of the men had an attack of appendicitis and an operation was imperative. Under primitive conditions the doctor saved his man and thwarted the growing pessimism in camp.

It was March now and the sun was fading. Soon the long winter night would descend on Little America. Precious time had disappeared and the success of Admiral Byrd's major project was endangered. This was "Advance Base," the admiral's program for studying weather conditions close to the South Pole.

Advance Base was to be the first manned base inland on the continent. Originally Byrd planned to winter there with several of his men and gather for the first time daily weather information, during the interior darkness. Back in Boston he had built a Mountain House to be transported to the polar plateau. But now as twilight thickened, he had to make two decisions.

First, it would be too dangerous to haul the Mountain House over the glaciers that cut through the Queen Maud Range to the polar plateau. It was even a gamble whether the portable weather station could be set at the foot of the Queen Mauds, for this was four hundred miles away. Byrd's final decision was to erect the Mountain House at a point almost one hundred and twenty-five miles from Little America. This point lay just before an unsafe area of mammoth crevasses.

Byrd's second decision concerned the occupants of the Mountain House. By the time March came, he reduced the number of possible tenants to three men. Then when he saw that it would not be possible to haul needed supplies for three, he considered two. But this idea he soon cast aside.

"Two men," he said, "jammed together at arm's length in a tiny shack in this strange environment, living by the dim light of a lantern in perpetual congestion and intrusion, staring at each other for seven months. The time comes when one has nothing left to reveal to the other, his pet ideas become a meaningless drool, and the way he blows out a lamp or drops his boots on the floor or eats his food becomes an annoyance. And this could happen between the best of friends."

Byrd's decision was to man the inland weather station alone, despite the protest of some of his associates. On March 16, he ordered the construction crew to begin its trek to Advance Base. Nine men traveled in four tractors in a journey below —50°F., with each mile menaced by blizzards and deep crevasses. On the twenty-first, they reached the site and despite frozen clothing and yellow frostbites, they put up Byrd's shack.

On the twenty-eighth, Byrd said farewell to the construction crew as they set off for Little America. It was almost dark now and the mercury was descending. The Mountain House was cold, said Byrd, but it "was as tidily built as a watch." The walls were made of plywood and the ceiling was bright aluminum. Underground tunnels held his stores. Inside his shack he had his bunk, a stove, scientific gear, and an excellent library. He had 360 pounds of meat and 792 pounds of vegetables. The shack lay under the surface, and only the stovepipe, weather instruments, and radio antennae protruded upward through the snow.

Byrd's normal routine kept him busy from eight o'clock in the morning until almost midnight. There were eight weather instruments to observe. Even though some worked mechanically, he had to keep them wound and check their operations. "The instruments were masters, not I," he admitted. At exactly 8 A.M., he climbed through the hatch and took a temperature reading. He also recorded at this time the percentage of cloudiness, amount of mist and snow drift, and the direction and speed of the wind. Not an hour went by during the rest of the day when there were not some readings to be taken. Byrd's outdoor weather observations were often made with the thermometer reading —80° or lower.

For safety reasons, Little America was able to communicate with Byrd at Advance Base by radio telephone. This was not a two-way system. In return, Byrd had to reply by Morse Code dots and dashes. A schedule of calls was set for 10 A.M. on Sundays, Tuesdays and Thursdays.

One of Byrd's shoulders had been painfully wrenched out of place during the construction of Advance Base. But this was a minor inconvenience compared with his major calamity. On May 6, almost six weeks after he began his solitary existence on the dark frozen wasteland, Byrd first noticed something was amiss. He wrote in his diary:

> I've been strangely irritable all day, and since supper have been depressed. I can't find any single thing to account for the mood. ... Tonight, for the first time, I must admit that the problem of keeping my mind on an even keel is a serious one.

There was good cause for his mood. The stovepipe section above the roof froze and prevented the release of poisonous fumes. In addition, his radio generator and defective oil stove poured carbon monoxide into his living quarters. On May 31, a crisis arose. He had been in touch with Little America when his radio generator acted poorly. "Wait," he signaled Little America, and then went into the snow tunnel to examine the generator.

The next thing he remembered was that he was on his hands and knees and slowly returning to consciousness. The poisoned upper air in the tunnel had felled him, but the cleaner air near the floor had revived him. Struggling, he crawled back into the shack. There was a sign-off signal to be sent Little America. Otherwise, the men there would grow concerned. He barely tapped out the necessary message on the key.

> My actions thereafter are uncertain [he wrote in his diary]. I really don't know which were nightmare and which were fact. I remember lying on the bunk, fully dressed, and hearing, as if with surprise, the irregular beat of the engine in the tunnel and realizing that I must shut it off to escape asphyxiation. Dizziness seized me, and my heart turned fantastic somersaults.

But he crawled back into the tunnel and turned off the ignition switch.

From this point on, Byrd fought a defensive battle against death. Splitting headaches lingered on and on; his eyes and brain pained; food brought on nausea. "I must sleep, I must sleep, something was saying inside me." Faintness overtook him at every move.

Yet he would not give up. Instead, he called upon strength he did not think he had to haul him up the ladder to make his outside readings. He crawled from task to task. Once when he was thirsty, he licked the snow in the tunnel until his tongue burned. "Death was a stranger sitting in a darkened room," he said of that period.

He would not inform Little America of his plight, and for good reason. His loyal men would have come after him and in the enveloping darkness several additional lives might have been lost. So no matter how wretched he felt, he religiously maintained his radio schedule with his home base. Each call left him utterly spent. He wrote on July 7:

> I am still in wretched condition. My brain seems unspeakably tired and confused. Last night was agony. This morning was one of my worst. The gloom, the cold and the evenness of the Barrier are a drag on the spirits; my poise and equanimity are almost gone.

By August, his men at Little America grew suspicious of his condition. His transmitted signals were often poor and frequently he broke in with "Wait," followed by long silence. Finally on August 8, a group set out by tractor to investigate.

Two days later the French horn on the machine let out a beep-beep-beep overhead. "Come on down, fellows," Byrd called out weakly. "I have a bowl of hot soup for you."

One of the men said afterward, "We were shocked at his appearance. Emaciated, hollow-cheeked, weak and haggard though he was, he met us casually, calmer by far than any of us . . . but his ghastly condition and husky voice told us that, in spite of this matter-of-factness, he had been through some terrific things." Yet his weather reports were complete.

Byrd had to remain at Advance Base two months before he had sufficient strength to return to Little America. In the meantime, three exploratory trail parties set out for the unknown that spring in September and October. By land and by air, some 200,000 square miles of new territories were discovered and charted. An extinct volcano lay on the path of one trail party. Another found several fossils and pieces of tree trunks, at a distance only 210 miles from the South Pole. Others uncovered ores such as lead and iron, and 94 species of plant life.

The biggest discovery turned out to be a practical joke. One man returned from the Queen Maud Range with a nugget of gold. Great excitement stirred Little America as the men planned an all-out search for the precious metal. Sheepishly the man with the nugget called a halt to the growing frenzy by disclosing that the gold was only a filling that had fallen from a tooth.

When Byrd recovered, he set out to prove or disprove that the Antarctic was in reality two continents. Little America sat on the edge of the high Ross Ice Shelf or Barrier. Although the Ross Ice Shelf appeared at first glance to be a part of the continent, in reality it was a floating piece of ice 500 miles long at the rim of the continent and 400 miles deep toward the South Pole. Some geologists claimed that a frozen strait connected the Ross Ice Shelf with a distant side of the continent. However, careful flights by Byrd in November, 1934, revealed that there was no strait cutting the Antarctic into pieces. Rimming the Shelf where the strait was supposed to be, he found a solid wall of land covered by ice. Antarctica was one continent, not two.

When Byrd returned to the United States in 1935, his old friend President Franklin D. Roosevelt came to the Washington Navy Yard to welcome him home. The President spoke of the expedition's "great achievement" in having added "valuable information in at least twenty-two separate branches of science." He also praised Byrd for having "filled in another large portion of the map of the world which has hitherto been a blank."

However, the President would not go a step further and stake out an American claim to those sections of the Antarctic Byrd had discovered. Byrd would have to be satisfied with the success of his expedition's explorations and scientific findings.

Chapter 10

ANTARCTIC COLONIES

ADMIRAL BYRD was fifty years old during October of 1938. The Antarctic deals cruelly with young men, as the admiral well knew. At his age, exploration should have been behind him—a set of maps and news stories pasted in a scrapbook. But the graying handsome man was far from finished. There was still so much to be done in and for the Antarctic, and no man was so able as he.

By 1939, several nations declared themselves to be owners of different sections of the Antarctic. Among these were Great Britain, New Zealand, Australia, France, Norway,

Chile, and Argentina. Most of the territory they claimed was still unseen or unmapped. Yet they claimed ownership.

The policy of the United States Government was to recognize none of these claims unless they were "followed by an actual settlement." However, when the Hitler Government of Nazi Germany announced that it, too, would make claims in the Antarctic, President Roosevelt grew concerned.

Roused to action now, he declared that it was time that the United States established its own claim to part of the Antarctic. And since his own government's rule was that no claim should be recognized without actual settlement, he proposed sending permanent colonies there. "Only Admiral Byrd can run such a program," he said. The result was that for the first time in a hundred years, the United States Government would support an Antarctic expedition.

Byrd was elated at the prospect of exploring with governmental backing. So when the U. S. Antarctic Service was established in the Department of the Interior, he became its commanding officer. Now there would be no problem in getting the one million dollars he needed to begin the American colonization of the Antarctic.

However, he was wrong. Congress refused to give more than $350,000 for a project that smacked of high adventure. Again he had to beg aid from other sources. From the War and Navy departments, he won use of supplies and equipment worth an additional $326,466. From his own bank account and from private backers, he raised another $240,000. He sold his icebreaker, the *Bear,* which he had overhauled at an expense of $120,000, to the Navy for one dollar.

The most expensive single gift to Byrd came from the Armour Institute in Chicago. This was the Snow Cruiser which cost $150,000. This vehicle measured 55 feet in length, 20 feet in width and stood 15 feet high, with wheels 10 feet in diameter. On top the Snow Cruiser was a small airplane, while inside it was a small but complete antarctic camp. Able to carry enough fuel to travel 5,000 miles, the crew of the Snow Cruiser planned a ride to the South Pole.

The directive from President Roosevelt to Admiral Byrd was clear-cut. He was to explore chiefly between 78 degrees west longitude and 148 degrees west. This was the area that extended from the antarctic zone beneath South America to approximately the Bay of Whales. President Roosevelt asked him to do so by long-range aerial flights equipped with mapping cameras to "consolidate these areas." There were also secondary geographical objectives, including the South Magnetic Pole and unknown areas on the far side of the Geographic South Pole. "Members of the Service," the President ordered, "may take any appropriate steps such as dropping written claims from airplanes, depositing such writings in cairns, et cetera, which might assist in supporting a sovereignty claim by the United States Government."

It was in the fall of 1939 that Byrd's two ships, the *Bear* and the *North Star,* an ancient vessel owned by the Department of the Interior, left the United States. Byrd was piped aboard the *North Star* at Panama for the long trip across the Pacific. A smile crossed his face as he gazed at the congestion, which included 65 Eskimo dogs, an enormous yellow plane, and the Snow Cruiser.

Despite his rank, Byrd asked for no special treatment. One day while he washed his clothes in a tub on deck, he found a sailor staring at him. He winked at the youth. "Didn't you ever see an admiral wash clothes?" he asked.

"No," replied the stammering sailor. "In fact, I never saw an admiral before."

The *North Star* reached New Zealand at the end of December. Here Byrd made up his mind to establish two permanent antarctic bases about 1,700 miles apart. He hoped to establish his West Base at a spot other than the Bay of Whales, where he had had so difficult a time unloading supplies on his second expedition. However, he could not locate a satisfactory landing place east of the bay and was forced to use it again.

Here Little America III was staked out close to Little America II, which lay in ruins from the violence of crunching pressure ice. The biggest job that January of 1940 was to bring the Snow Cruiser to the top of the barrier wall. Though the Snow Cruiser had acted superbly in tests back in the United States, it became a total failure in the Antarctic. It could not climb hills of snow. After groaning for three miles, the Snow Cruiser died a sad death.

Byrd left West Base in the capable hands of his assistant, Dr. Paul A. Siple. In 1928 Siple had won the contest among 600,000 Boy Scouts to accompany Byrd on his first expedition. A brawny giant, Siple was also a noted polar geographer and explorer. This was his third expedition to the Antarctic.

From West Base Byrd moved eastward on the *Bear* for

some exploration and in search of an adequate place for East Base. Along the way, he discovered many new places on the coastline both from the ship and from airplanes. Byrd hoped to set East Base on Charcot Island where no man had ever landed. However, this did not prove possible because of a solid ice belt. Byrd finally settled for a site farther east on the Palmer Peninsula, which points upward toward South America. Here he named Richard B. Black, who had served on his second expedition, as base commander.

With both bases in capable hands, Byrd returned to the United States in March, 1940. Here from afar, he guided the destiny of the two colonies. This was not a simple task, he was to find out, because emergency after emergency hit both bases. For example, on June 7 during the winter night at West Base, a fire broke out that endangered the lives of all the dogs. Despite a temperature of −50° and a howling blizzard, the men worked frantically to save the animals. During the fire the camp's electrical system failed. Yet by heroics all the dogs were rescued, even though some were already unconscious.

There was also a near tragedy on July 26 when a man set out lightly clad from West Base to commit suicide. Byrd had never lost a man on his various expeditions and he pressed for a full search. Two days later, after the man was given up for dead, he crawled back to camp. His body was given to convulsive shivering and he was so dry that he could not quench his thirst for hours. Along the way he had decided to stay alive and, though lost, luck brought him back to camp.

Both bases accomplished extraordinary explorations.

One group completed an aerial field map of a region as large as Connecticut. Total explorations covered more than one million square miles of Antarctica. Geologists found copper, molybdenum, manganese, and bituminous coal. Other scientists discovered that the icecap over the continent—in some places two miles thick—moved steadily from the plateau where the South Pole lay to the distant seas. It poured like lava from the Pole across mountains and valleys at a relentless rate of four feet each day. At the edge of the continent, the ice "calved," or broke off thunderously into mammoth icebergs.

By the end of the first year, the settlers were comfortably adjusted to their way of life. On all the treks, Byrd's orders were carefully followed and American flags, claim sheets and bronze benchmark monuments denoted American claims. Two men at East Base walked 1,200 miles in 84 days.

However, instead of feeling elation Byrd was sad. Cutting requirements to the bone, he asked Congress for $250,000 to maintain his two bases for another year. President Roosevelt also supported this request, but World War II already raged in Europe and Asia, and Congress would not appropriate further.

As a result, the U. S. Antarctic Service was abandoned. With this action, Byrd's dream of a permanent American program in the Antarctic temporarily came to an end.

Chapter 11

THE WAR AND HIGHJUMP

ALTHOUGH Admiral Byrd was fifty-three years old when the United States became directly involved in World War II, he was quick to offer his services to President Roosevelt. The President did not hesitate to accept his help and sent him off on several highly secret missions.

These ranged from advising on polar clothing for the Armed Forces to forays on the battlefields. From his experiences in both the Arctic and the Antarctic, Byrd was perhaps best qualified to tell how machines, wearing apparel and men would react in the cold. From experiments he knew that at —50°F. a kerosene lamp won't work; touching metal with bare skin would produce a burn similar to fire. His development of a cotton outer garment called Byrd Cloth was proof that light clothing could protect a person from the cold as well as clumsy and heavy wool or fur. His constant nagging of airplane engineers and designers to produce for him better planes for exploring aided directly in the development of military planes.

However, it was as a keen observer, planner, and daredevil that his services were most valued. Long before American Marines landed at the heavily fortified Japanese stronghold at Guadalcanal in August of 1942, Byrd conducted a pre-attack inspection of that island for the Navy. He also surveyed more than thirty other islands in the Pacific, many of which had never before been mapped.

President Roosevelt utilized Byrd in still other directions. On one occasion he was sent to New Zealand to help co-ordinate that country's war program with that of the United States. Once back home again, Byrd drew up a strategic over-all plan for the Pacific fighting at the request of the President and Admiral Ernest J. King, Commander of the U. S. Fleet. Among Byrd's chief points was one urging the United States to use the Antarctic as a strategic supply base. Specifically he advocated establishing a base at Deception Island in Antarctica below South America. Deception Island had one of the best natural harbors in the world. In fact, as Byrd pointed out, German submarines used this harbor to maneuver quickly into the Atlantic and Pacific oceans.

In 1944, when the Allied Forces invaded Europe, Admiral Byrd went to France. Here his mission was to study how to improve combined air and ground fighting. On one occasion he flew thirty-five miles in a low swoop behind enemy lines to observe German operations. Though anti-aircraft guns peppered the air with flak, he nonchalantly completed his study and returned undamaged. When the European fighting ended, he flew to the Orient. Here, after Japan surrendered, he completed his last government mission, which was to inspect the atom bomb damage to Hiroshima and Nagasaki.

Once the war was over, it was natural that his thoughts would turn again to the Antarctic. This time he approached Secretary of the Navy James V. Forrestal and Fleet Admiral Chester W. Nimitz, and sold them on the broadest attack yet on the ice continent. Through war developments, he argued, the Navy now had excellent long-range aircraft, icebreakers and a variety of amphibious machines. Why let all of these sit idle? Why not test them in the Antarctic? Since the United States had emerged from the war with farflung world-wide interests, the Antarctic had new importance. It lay in the center of the road connecting Asia, Africa, and South America.

Forrestal and Nimitz were quick to agree. Instead of being remote, the Antarctic had suddenly acquired vital strategic importance. On August 26, 1946, they issued a directive naming Admiral Byrd as Officer in Charge of a new attack on the Antarctic. The original title of the new operation was Operation Polevault. But when some said this sounded as if the United States planned to "capture" the South Pole, the title was changed to Operation Highjump.

The directive to Byrd was quite sweeping. He would train men and test equipment under polar conditions. There would also be a variety of scientific programs, ranging from studies of weather to geomagnetism. He was also to determine whether it was possible to build an air base for the Navy's heavy planes "with particular attention to later application of such techniques to operations in interior Greenland." However, dearest to Byrd's heart was one provision for "consolidating and extending United States sovereignty over the largest practicable area of the Antarctic continent."

Admiral Byrd was intent on getting Highjump into operation that year. For he knew that Congress might not appropriate money the following year for such an undertaking. However, the best flying weather in the Antarctic came during the months of November and December. This gave him precious little time to lay his plans and gather together his men and equipment. How much work he had to accomplish can be shown by the dimensions of his undertaking.

He planned on taking thirteen ships and 4,200 men to the Antarctic. Of his ships, one was the mammoth aircraft carrier, the *Philippine Sea*. He also counted on bringing a submarine, the *Sennet,* to test its ability to get through the ice pack. His command ship, the *Mount Olympus,* contained three radio rooms with space for fifty radio operators. For aerial work, Byrd acquired four helicopters and nineteen airplanes. Indeed, this was to be the biggest assault in history on the Antarctic.

In early December, Byrd's fleet got under way. The line of attack was clear. Two task forces would sail in opposite directions to explore the 16,000-mile coastline of what Byrd called "an enchanted continent in the sky, like a pale sleeping beauty." Meanwhile, Byrd's central group of four ships would head for the Bay of Whales. Here Little America IV would be built and an airfield hewn from the rough ice surface. Then ski-equipped land planes would photograph the continent's interior with newly developed three-lensed cameras that took contour and elevation pictures.

Many crises developed on the trip down. The submarine *Sennet* was so battered and dented by the ice pack that she had to be towed out to clear water. As for the other ships heading toward the Bay of Whales, all were damaged. Especially disappointing was the pounding taken by the *Northwind,* a newly developed icebreaker type with a thin steel shell. For two wild weeks the central Highjump fleet fought the ice pack before getting through. On some days the ice actually carried them backward six miles and more. Then when the Bay of Whales was reached, the two open sides of the high barrier wall had come together and the bay was no longer in existence. However, the *Northwind* redeemed herself by smashing fifteen million tons of hard ice in only three days, so the other ships could drop anchor.

Admiral Byrd traveled on the 35,000-ton aircraft carrier, *Philippine Sea.* Even on this enormous vessel, he soon learned, "icebergs and heavy pack are to a thin-skinned aircraft carrier as dangerous as rocks." The carrier could not possibly plow through the six hundred miles of pack ice to Little America. If he were to reach the continent, he would have to fly.

The great unknown was "Can we do it?" For the planes

on the carrier were the largest ones ever carried by such a vessel. None had ever undergone a test flight from the carrier deck. Besides, the normal runway requirement was 2,500 feet for the big R4D planes; and the wide wingspread of the planes prevented the use of more than 400 feet of the flight deck.

After careful calculations Byrd concluded that a successful take-off was possible. If JATO bottles, or rocket-propulsion tubes the size of fire extinguishers, were attached to the bottom of the fuselage the thrust might shoot the plane aloft on the short runway. Several officers aboard the carrier doubted the wisdom of this experiment, but Byrd was certain it would work.

So on January 29, 1947, he and his crew climbed into their Douglas Skytrain and waved farewell to their carrier friends. The plane was pointed at an angle off the center strip so that if it plummeted into the sea the carrier would not run over it. Byrd had calculated that the safest take-off would come when the *Philippine Sea* was traveling at thirty knots. And when he felt the vibrations that told him the ship was moving along at that speed, he knew it was time for the plane to depart. "We seemed to creep along the deck at first, and it looked as if we could never make it with only 400 feet. . . . But when our four JATO bottles went off with a terrific, deafening noise I could see the deck fall away. I knew that we had made it."

The flight itself, spanning 800 miles, held no further adventures except for a dangerous landing at storm-tossed Little America. Here a tent camp for three hundred men had arisen near the edge of the barrier wall, nine miles north of Little America I of 1929. A close look at the barrier surface and Byrd realized that it would not be too long before Little America IV would float out to sea. But it was his intention not to tarry here for longer than six weeks to complete his program. For then the dark winter night would be on its way and a tent village would not be able to survive.

It was a disappointment to him that the weather was not sufficiently safe for flying until February 13. This curtailed drastically his air-mapping time, yet he hoped to make up for it by longer and more intensive flights. Actually his goal of twenty-five single-plane flights was exceeded by four, with the photographing planes spending 220 hours in the air and covering 27,500 miles.

With only two good flying weeks, Byrd and his men photographed more than 200,000 square miles. "We discovered literally hundreds of mountains and hundreds of mountain peaks never before seen by man," he reported. "Some of these had elevations of at least 15,000 feet." He estimated that one newly found mountain range was 20,000 feet high, making it among the highest in the world. Among his 70,000 photos, one could piece together almost the entire outer edge of the continent.

One of Byrd's goals was to explore by air the great unknown section of Antarctica beyond the South Pole. Almost at midnight on February 15, Byrd left Little America to examine what lay there. The sun was a large red wheel that rolled along the horizon. Looking down on the continent, Byrd saw the wind-ridged surface, which was shiny white with gold and blue tinges. Crevasses miles long had chasms that looked purple and blue. Mountaintops were clear of snow and were either coal black or brick red.

Passing over the glaciers that cut across the Queen Maud Range, one of the plane's engines stopped. But Byrd calmly attached it to another gas tank and it started up again. Once across Maud and onto the high polar plateau, Byrd rode the 180th Meridian straight toward the Pole. At 13,000 feet, the plane moved forward at 130 miles an hour some 2,000 feet above the ice plateau. The lack of sufficient oxygen at that height brought on anoxia among the crew and produced staggering walk and fumbling speech.

Within a few hours the plane was over the Pole and Byrd gazed down upon the white surface that was tinged with gold as the sun hit it. Then he dropped a cardboard box containing the flags of all the members of the United Nations. After this ceremony the plane went on about one hundred miles into the unknown before turning back to Little America. What he glimpsed beyond the Pole, he reported, was that "there was no observable feature of any significance. There was only the rolling white desert from horizon to horizon."

On February 23, Little America had to be evacuated. The planes had to be abandoned there because there was no way to get them out. Yet though he always hated waste, Byrd knew that the loss was worth the effort.

For the government now seemed thoroughly interested in the Antarctic after his long years of efforts to achieve this goal. It had proved itself as a testing ground for men and machines. It provided a fertile field for scientific research not possible anywhere else on earth. More than ever he was convinced that the Antarctic was "actually a treasure house of fabulous riches." Most important, he believed he was nearer his dream of establishing an American claim to most of the Antarctic.

Chapter 12

DEEP FREEZE

WHEN Admiral Byrd returned to the United States
after Operation Highjump, he immediately em-
barked on a new project that he called Highjump II.
Through Highjump I, he pointed out, the United States
had a fairly detailed picture of the coast of Antarctica. Now
through a follow-up operation, the interior of the continent could be similarly exposed.

"No other country is capable of doing this immense job," he said enthusiastically to the Secretary of the Navy. "And if we do it, we will have the leading claim over most of the Antarctic."

The Navy quickly gave its assent to Operation Highjump II and Byrd boldly plunged into details of men and equipment. He brought together trusted and skilled aides from previous expeditions, requisitioned swift and powerful planes.

Ships and captains were ready to sail when he received devastating news. The White House had suddenly called off Highjump II on the ground that the government wanted to cut its spending. "But the money is already spent," Byrd argued. "We have already bought and paid for our supplies." Though this was true, he could not persuade the government to change its mind. Once again, as it had so many times in the past, victory eluded him just when it appeared to be in his grasp.

In 1948, Byrd reached his sixtieth birthday. Throughout the world he was known as the Admiral of the Antarctic, though he knew that he would never rest until he reached his goal. For the first time his associates grew concerned with his relentless drive, for his general health had grown slowly worse.

By now in the Antarctic, France, Britain, New Zealand, Norway, and Australia agreed to recognize each other's broad claims within the Antarctic. As salve for the United States, these countries agreed to recognize American ownership over a small piece of the continent facing the Pacific Ocean. This was a stretch of the Antarctic that no ship

had ever been able to reach because the outlying ice pack
was thick and never melted.

Byrd could not sit idly by and watch his life's work go
down an icy drain. With dogged persistence he button-
holed various government officials to do something about
this situation. All this effort finally paid off in the early
1950's when the U. S. Department of State grew concerned.
"We need a ten-year program in the Antarctic," officials
told Byrd. "First we need a written history of all your
activities and discoveries there. Second, we'll have to complete the mapping and exploring you originally planned
for Operation Highjump II."

Elated, Byrd began preparing meticulous details. This
would be the final effort to establish American claims in
the Antarctic. He would have permanent bases there to
renew again the effort of his U. S. Antarctic Service colonies of 1939–1941. Now nothing would stand in his way
of claiming a continent for his country. It would be his
legacy to the country he loved.

In the midst of his hard work, another program affecting
the Antarctic came into existence. This was the Interna-
tional Geophysical Year, or IGY. Geophysicists, who study
the physical aspects of the earth and its atmosphere, such
as weather, astronomy, magnetism, gravity, the aurora, the
ionosphere, earthquakes and cosmic rays, hoped to stage a
world-wide study during 1957–1958. This would be the
time when enormous storms on the sun would produce a
peak of sunspots, the most suitable period for probing the
geophysical sciences. And since sunspot activities had
greater effect on the earth's physical happenings in polar

regions than elsewhere, the IGY program hoped to concentrate most heavily in the Antarctic.

If scientists were to do their observing in the Antarctic,
bases would have to be built to house them and their instruments. Twelve nations were planning IGY stations in
the Antarctic. President Eisenhower officially appointed
Byrd as Officer in Charge of the U. S. Antarctic Program.
In addition to his national political program in the Antarctic, Byrd would also take command of the scientific program run by the IGY. As Admiral Arleigh Burke, Chief
of Naval Operations, noted, Byrd was to be "the senior
U. S. representative charged with maintaining effective
monitorship over those political, scientific, legislative and
operational activities which comprise the over-all U. S.
Antarctic Programs."

The IGY program complicated Byrd's task, but as a
pioneer in antarctic science he realized its importance. Besides, some of the stations established for IGY scientists
could be maintained as permanent American bases after
the IGY program ended.

Byrd now conceived a carefully planned series of antarctic operations. The first one, called Deep Freeze I, would
go into effect during the antarctic summer of November,
1955, to March, 1956. During this time some of the seven
American IGY stations would be established. Supplies
would be delivered for the erection of other IGY stations
during a future Deep Freeze II. Also, a Navy support base
would be established at McMurdo Sound at the continent's
edge, 400 miles west of the Bay of Whales. Here on Ross
Island close to the most lively volcano in the Antarctic, the

13,200-foot-high Mount Erebus, Captain Scott had set out for his ill-fated trip to the South Pole. Now Ross Island in McMurdo Sound would serve the Navy as a jumping-off base for building an IGY station at the South Pole itself.

In November of 1955, the ships of Deep Freeze I got under way for the Antarctic. Byrd planned to fly to New Zealand where he would meet the newest American ice-breaker, the *Glacier,* and travel on her to McMurdo Sound. Friends noticed that the many irritations involved in putting Deep Freeze I into operation had startlingly undermined his health. His hair was now white, his cheeks were sunken and he had lost several pounds. Yet his eyes were still bright blue and he walked with perfect military posture.

In New Zealand, Byrd was treated royally, with the Air Force marching in a dress parade in his honor. But responding to crowds at banquet tables and at ceremonies tired him. So did the long voyage through the ice pack. For the *Glacier* was built with a round bottom and she shook so violently when she encountered ice that her men were tossed about as if they were toys.

At McMurdo Sound, the *Glacier* stopped, close to a pack of killer whales. Fortunately they did not bother the men who swarmed off the icebreaker to erect a camp on Ross Island and an 8,000-foot airstrip on thick bay ice. A safe airstrip was essential to Byrd's plans, for heavy planes flying 2,000 miles nonstop from New Zealand required a smooth landing zone. Ever concerned about the safety of his men, he breathed with relief when the first four planes completed their historic flight.

In the McMurdo area he encountered mute evidence of the explorers who had preceded him. On Ross Island, Scott's base camp of his 1901–1904 expedition was still in good condition. Again Byrd was impressed with the wonders of the Antarctic. A rope near Scott's 30-foot-square hut was as good as new. The nails pounded into the shack held no rust. Matches left by Scott's men lighted easily. But the most unusual sight was that of a Husky dog who stood upright completely preserved close by the hut. Frozen all these years, he looked alive and ready for a long pull.

With the McMurdo Sound naval base and airstrip in preliminary operation, Byrd moved on to the establishment of Little America V some 400 miles eastward. Here the Bay of Whales no longer existed, and instead a high solid barrier wall confronted him. Nevertheless, he felt homesick for a sight of Little America I and went on a helicopter flight to the scene of his first attack on the Antarctic. The camp now lay dozens of feet below the surface. In fact, the three 70-foot steel radio towers he had planted in 1929 now stood less than ten feet above snow.

With the Bay of Whales gone, the site of Little America V had to be shifted to the Kainan Bay inlet about twenty miles to the east. Here Byrd came ashore to attend the flag-raising ceremony. Dressed on purpose in the explorer's garb he had worn on his first expedition, he represented the link between those early days and current exploration.

Back at McMurdo again, he was confronted with bad news. A Marine pilot engaged in mapping the interior of the continent had flown over the South Pole. On his return he insisted that the snow at the Pole was so deep that any airplanes attempting a landing would sink and disappear. Many on Byrd's planning staff were shocked by this news. "This eliminates a South Pole station," they said.

However, Byrd knew from his own flights over the Pole that the snow had not appeared soft from the air. In addition, both Amundsen and Scott had walked across the Pole. Nevertheless, to put an end to the fears of his staff, he found it necessary to make another flight there.

Byrd hoped to make the first plane landing in history at the South Pole. Here he could examine the surface closely and make vital scientific observations that would ease the task of those who would later build a South Pole station. However, his planes had wheels and were not equipped with skis. Disappointed in his own lack of foresight in not bringing along a ski-equipped plane, he had to settle for a flight over the polar plateau. "The South Pole doesn't look any different from the way it did on my 1929 and 1947 flights," he said upon his return. "It is safe for ski-equipped planes to land there."

When Byrd returned to the United States from Deep Freeze I in the spring of 1956, the task of preparing for Deep Freeze II began. This new expedition would begin late that year and would put the IGY Antarctic stations into operation.

Slowly but steadily Byrd's health continued to decline. All the while, he grew increasingly concerned with the problems involved in maintaining a station at the South Pole. For here the temperature might drop to $-130°$F. and the winter night is six months long. Also, situated on a two-mile-high ice plateau, the Pole's oxygen supply at that altitude would be rare. If anything extraordinary happened at the Pole during the dark winter night, there would be no way to fly in aid.

The experience would truly be similar to that of living on another planet. Establishing and maintaining a base at the Pole would have been a high point in Byrd's adventurous career. But he could not make the trip. Instead, he insisted that Paul Siple, his lieutenant on his five Antarctic expeditions, undertake this responsibility. "Since I can't go," he told Siple, "there is no one else I'd rather see taking my place than you."

When Siple left Byrd, he had the strange foreboding that he would never see Byrd again. Byrd's eyes were moist as he said farewell.

That fall as Deep Freeze II got under way, Admiral Byrd remained in close touch with its many activities, though his strength ebbed more rapidly now.

Early on March 11, 1957, he sent a message to Paul Siple at the South Pole. "Delighted to learn all men safely at Pole and nearly all supplies in. Please convey my wholehearted congratulations to all hands at Station on their part in this splendid achievement."

Late that day as the Boston sun was setting, Byrd lay in bed asleep. With his wife and four children standing close by, he died at 6:20 P.M.

At the South Pole, a saddened group of explorers lowered their flag to half-mast and the howling wind flapped it wildly. In Washington, the President said that a close friend had departed. And throughout the world millions felt the loss of a daring and adventurous soul who had rolled back unknown frontiers into more distant horizons and let more sunlight in.

Said *The New York Times* about a rare breed of man: "They are men of the world; the sort of men who carry the world forward, who open horizons, who make a mark on history's pages that can never be erased. Richard E. Byrd was such a man."